Economic Diplomacy and Foreign Policy-making

Charles Chatterjee

Economic Diplomacy and Foreign Policy-making

palgrave
macmillan

Charles Chatterjee
Institute of Advanced Legal Studies
University of London
London, UK

ISBN 978-3-030-49046-1 ISBN 978-3-030-49047-8 (eBook)
https://doi.org/10.1007/978-3-030-49047-8

This Palgrave Macmillan imprint is published by the registered company Springer Nature Switzerland AG
The registered company address is: Gewerbestrasse 11, 6330 Cham, Switzerland

Introduction

Economic/Commercial diplomacy is at the root of foreign policy-making by States; the importance of military diplomacy or diplomacy of security may not be denied, but if one takes "peace-making" seriously, then one should be able to establish one's own hierarchy of diplomacies. Economic/commercial diplomacy is so crucially important in making friendship with other States and inter-State rapport that a State would reject it at its own peril. Indeed, the interplay between this type of diplomacy and foreign policy-making has become intertwined.[1]

Pigman maintains that commercial/economic diplomacy which has a very long and impressive history existed even before many of the current States were born.[2] Economic/commercial diplomacy is not only concerned with providing negotiating techniques in inter-State trade and investment, policy-making but also with development of framework legislation addressed to the international community.

[1] K. S. Rana, *21st Century Diplomacy*, The Continuum International Publishing Group (2011).

[2] G. Pigman, *Contemporary Diplomacy*, London Polity Press (2010).

The terms "economic diplomacy" and "commercial diplomacy" are often interchangeably used,[3] but they stand for two purposes, and yet share certain common features. According to Sridharan, commercial diplomacy is an aspect of economic diplomacy.[4] It might be appropriate to maintain that economic diplomacy is broader in scope than commercial diplomacy, the latter is predominantly concerned with inter-state trade and transactions, but these interactions are usually based on bi-lateral treaties between the two States concerned; on the other hand, those who would prefer the term "commercial diplomacy" would also include the attributes of "economic diplomacy" in it. The controversy surrounding these two terms may be never-ending; according to Ruel:

> "... commercial diplomacy is the international relations of business that knits together political and entrepreneurial activities and agents in the global market."[5]

According to Lee and Ruel, commercial diplomacy primarily focuses on developing networks of diplomats and commercial groups to promote trade and investment.[6] As to economic diplomacy, Hann maintains that economic diplomacy is an effective tool to achieve economic and foreign policy goals.[7] Naray considers commercial diplomacy as a vital part of economic diplomacy.[8] In other words, economic diplomacy is wider in scope than commercial diplomacy. Rana believes that economic diplomacy is a process utilised to establish rapport with the wider world,

[3] H. Ruel, *Commercial Diplomacy and International Business: A Conceptual and Empirical Exploration*, Emerald Group Publishing Ltd (2012); see also M. I. Ozdem, *Governmental Agencies in Commercial Diplomacy: Seeking the Optional Agency Structure for Foreign Trade Policy*, Raleigh, North Carolina State University (2009).

[4] K. Sridharan, "Commercial Diplomacy and Statecraft in the Context of Economic Reform: The Indian Experience," *Diplomacy and Statecraft*, vol. 13(2) 57–82.

[5] H Ruel, *Commercial Diplomacy and International Business: A Conceptual and Empirical Exploration*, Emerald Group (2012) at 15.

[6] D. Lee and H. Ruel, 'Introduction: Commercial Diplomacy and International Business' in H. Ruel (ed.) *Commercial Diplomacy and International Business: A Conceptual and Empirical Exploration*, (2012) at 15.

[7] H. Maull (ed.), *Germany's Uncertain Power: Foreign Policy of the Berlin Republic (New Perspectives in German Political Studies)*, London, Palgrave Macmillan (2006).

[8] O. Naray, Commercial Diplomacy: A Conceptual Overview: A Paper presented at the 7th World Conference of TPOS, *The Hague* (2008).

and to maximise their national gains in all fields of activity, including trade, investment and other forms of economically beneficial exchanges.[9] On the other hand, commercial diplomacy may gradually be graduated to economic diplomacy—the latter contains elements of commercial diplomacy.

Controversies aside, it may be pointed out that both commercial diplomacy and economic diplomacy aim at meaningful "reciprocity" between chosen States based on bi-lateral treaties. This issue has received further attention in Chapter 12. Such reciprocities may not be established unless the States concerned surrender part of their "functional" sovereignty.

Economic diplomacy should be clean, ethical and a benefit-maximising process; it forms the basis for true co-operation between States as well as forming the foundation of socio-economic development. It should not be viewed only as a vehicle of acquiring financial aid, technology by developing countries from developed countries. Developing countries, either directly or through their Missions in various developed States, can also develop good rapport with the latter by offering them sustainable proposals, for example, BOT (Build, Operate and Transfer) whereby on the basis of a developing country's invitation a relevant corporate entity from the developed receiving State will agree to set up a factory for manufacturing certain goods which would have a good market demand in that receiving State. The result would be beneficial for both the receiving State and the sending State. In this process whereas the company from the receiving State will be able to manufacture products at a cheaper cost, the materials and labour being provided for by the sending State, the latter's people, as part of the contractual terms, will have the training and skills to manufacture that product for which export markets will usually be created by the receiving State's corporate entity (this process may also be described as an aspect of "capacity building"). This way, both countries benefit, and the dependency of countries on other countries diminishes. Teaching with the participation of foreign teachers, is a technique, of capacity building too. Sophistication of the manufacturing process of industrial products may also be achieved by developing countries by this method too. There are certain other disciplines too, namely, tropical medicines, history or geography or exploration and exploitation of natural resources, development of investment legislation, or transform

[9] K. S. Rana, *21st Century Diplomacy* (2011) op. cit.

the local judiciary into a sophisticated one or development of any other relevant legislation in relation to banking, insurance, shipping etc. are but a few examples in which the technique of "capacity building" may be applied. In this process both the parties to an arrangement benefit. Advanced knowledge in science and technology may also be gained by this process.

Economic/commercial diplomacy is the closest form of diplomacy for achieving socio-economic development in a country; this form of development should not admit of any "politics"—a diplomat engaged in economic/commercial diplomacy must be a person possessing knowledge and experience in various disciplines—geography, history, international trade policy-making, techniques required for negotiating bi-lateral reciprocal contracts, amongst others.

The scope of economic diplomacy which has received attention in a separate chapter of this work is virtually unlimited. The perceptions of diplomats as to the ramifications of this discipline determines its scope. The relationship between science and technology and economic/commercial diplomacy, which was not given much importance in the past, has proved to be important. Economic diplomacy is a business-relationship diplomacy, one of the important purposes of which is to identify the nature of "synergy" at a bi-lateral level. It must be progressive but not "galloping" in its speed. The countries concerned must develop their capacity to absorb and adapt. Its objective is to develop meaningful reciprocity, but not dependency. Meaningful economic/commercial diplomacy may be developed between two countries of unequal level, initially, at a narrow level, gradually and eventually in an effective way.

Economic diplomacy should work at three levels: national, regional and international; at each level, the technique of diplomacy varies. One of the objectives of economic diplomacy is economic globalisation; but the latter cannot be achieved only by the former; hence the need for international co-operation based on an appropriate understanding of what economic globalisation stands for.

Economic diplomacy has often been highly politicised; this work's principal theme is to progress with this form of diplomacy by friendly means, rather than subdued by the stronger powers, and establish sensible reciprocity; diplomats may find UN guidelines provided by its various offices in the form of Declarations, Recommendations, Resolutions and Conventions, which are very useful in negotiating reciprocity at both bi-lateral and multilateral levels.

This works has been developed principally by referring to the relevant primary sources of information; secondary sources of information have been referred to whenever necessary.

Contents

CHAPTER 1

The Nature of Economic Diplomacy and Foreign Policy-Making

The primary objective of economic diplomacy at a national level is to reach mutually beneficial arrangements the spill-over effect of which strengthens the foreign policy relations between the two States concerned. Economic diplomacy at an international level should aim at developing framework regulations whether in the form of international conventions or resolutions or declarations, etc. The tactics and strategies at these two levels of diplomacy are different. Whereas bi-lateral economic diplomacy requires to protect mutually beneficial national economic interest by identifying the bases for reciprocity between the parties concerned, economic diplomacy carried out at an international level is not concerned with deriving any reciprocal benefit for anybody; its main objective is to achieve something for the entire international community.

Whereas the nature of tactics and strategies of bi-lateral economic diplomacy primarily relate to the strengths and weaknesses of the parties, without surrendering one to the other, economic diplomacy at a truly international level should be visionary—it requires a thorough understanding of the needs for framework regulations; it is not concerned with the objective of protecting the national interest of any kind. Diplomats must be able to justify why a new framework convention or regulation would be necessary. It is not based on any selfish ideas. Whereas "tactics" stands for the "plans and means adopted in carrying out a scheme

C. Chatterjee, *Economic Diplomacy and Foreign Policy-making*,
https://doi.org/10.1007/978-3-030-49047-8_1

or achieving some end" or a skilful device or devices,[1] a "strategy" stands for a "plan of action or policy in business".[2] Both tactics and strategies require a thorough understanding of the issues and problems relating to the subject matter of diplomacy.

In so far as economic diplomacy at a domestic level is concerned, all negotiations should centre around the national interest, but combining it with the other party's beneficial interest too. In other words, reciprocity between the two parties must be highlighted; however reciprocal interests may not be exactly balanced if both the parties are not of similar standing. In other words, in such circumstances "reciprocity" may not be perceived in its absolute form. This issue assumes particular importance when one of the parties to an economic diplomacy manoeuvre is a developing country. The objective of economic diplomacy is not only to create and maintain economic and commercial relationship between the two parties but also to develop "capacity building" with a view to strengthening the economic and commercial foundations including infrastructures of a country. In negotiating economic and commercial deals on a State to State basis, which should eventually take the form of a bi-lateral treaty between the two parties concerned, if one of the parties is a developing country, it should also negotiate a "capacity building" plan as an integral part of such a deal. It is through economic diplomacy that "economic dependence" on countries should be minimised, which should eventually allow the developing country to attain a competitive status.

Although decolonisation process started in the late 1940s, it was not until the 1990s that the concept of "capacity building" was really promoted by the international community. In economic diplomacy-based negotiations, the parties should ideally be treated as "partners" instead of "contracting parties". However unbusinesslike it may sound, the more capable party should develop confidence in the minds of the less capable rather than treating it with "pity".

Economic diplomacy is a dynamic concept in that it must be creative, innovative and inventive. People engaged in economic diplomacy must also possess the same qualities to be able to rise to its demands. Economic diplomacy is at its worst when it is operated on a false perception of bargaining power of the parties concerned. At the core of diplomacy is the

[1] See *Oxford Modern English Dictionary*, Oxford, Clarendon Press (1992) at 1133.

[2] Op. cit., at 1081.

art of negotiation, and in that art, there is no room for "muscle power"; instead, it represents the power to negotiate, which is nothing but inventive and innovative power of the actors. If it is to be based on "muscle power" and the "power to dominate" one by the other, then there would be no room for negotiation—it is otiose.

Economic diplomacy should not necessarily be anecdotal. Historic ties with countries may be a contributory factor for carrying on economic and commercial diplomacy between themselves, but it has its disadvantages too—it may consolidate into what may be described as diplomacy of dependency. After achieving their self-determination (decolonised sovereign States) the former colonies have in many cases stayed with their respective colonial masters in the belief that "rapport" would be more meaningful between them, which perception may be sustainable, but there is no harm in adopting a truly international outlook in expanding their economic and commercial activities. Cross-fertilisation of economic diplomacy may provide new opportunities, innovative ideas and competitive prices and advantages; this is, of course, not to suggest that the newly born countries should not develop any economic and commercial diplomacy and relationship with their former colonial masters. Economic diplomacy must derive benefits from as many sources as possible as it must also be as worldwide as possible.

As development stands for socio-economic development, human resource development is to be regarded as one of the main objectives of economic diplomacy too. Thus, economic diplomacy should be directed at knowledge-building with the help of others which would eventually lead to a knowledge-based economy, as without any creative knowledge there will be no solid foundation of a country. Diplomats should not therefore take a myopic view of economic diplomacy. It has already been stated that without an effective interacting economic diplomacy between countries, general inter-State diplomacy will have a fragile foundation; the examples of developing countries sufficiently evidentiary of this statement.

Without any effective reciprocity between the partner countries, there may not be any successful and long-lasting economic relationship between them. Economic diplomacy showed this progress through stages: initially, almost "unilateral"—seeking help from the developed by the developing countries, and gradually, through the learning—knowledge-building process, proper reciprocal arrangements will be effective. Although during the initial period, economic diplomacy between a developed and developing country is almost unilateral, a degree of reciprocity may nonetheless be imported into the process by providing some services or materials, determined by the parties themselves as well as by the developing country concerned.

The above-mentioned point deserves further attention because, historically, since the decolonisation days, in the name of economic diplomacy, majority of the developing countries tend to reciprocate with developed countries at the expense of their natural resources which policy should be urgently reviewed and reconsidered. Natural resources and human resources are the best form of wealth that a country may have. Economic diplomacy between two developed countries is usually based on a high degree of reciprocity and such reciprocity proves to be beneficial for both parties by virtue of their having effectively engaged in mutual sharing of knowledge and building of new knowledge. This is one of the reasons why effective knowledge-based resource building between two developed countries takes place at almost all relevant levels including educational and scientific research programmes between universities in their countries.

On the other hand, economic diplomacy between two developing countries of similar economic standing at a bi-lateral level can also be interesting and effective. Joint programmes of socio-economic development with the assistance of a developed country may prove to be useful and cost-effective. Economic diplomacy is not all about developing rapport with developed countries or other countries for creating the scope of export trade; it should be effectively utilised for internal socio-economic development of a country. The stronger a country at the level of socio-economic level, the better.

Regional economic diplomacy in various regions of the world has become proactive particularly over the past five decades or so although its origin may be traced in the Zollverein in Germany or the Benelux Union or the Nordic Council before the current regional economic integrations came into being. Regional economic integrations have their merits as well as disadvantages, and diplomacy between regional economic integrations or between them and the non-member countries have certain special features and characteristics which have received attention in a separate chapter of this work. The crucial point for diplomats to consider whether regional economic integrations hinder trade liberalisation process in the world whereby not all countries may have market access to integrated markets even though their products are of the required standards and competitive in price.

Economic diplomacy has yet another dimension—its full play at an international level with a view to discussing matters of "concern" in relation to international economic issues. At such platforms (ECOSOC, WTO, UNCTAD and UNIDO, etc.) diplomats must develop framework agreements and eventually binding conventions. Economic diplomacy is not merely concerned with negotiations of commercial issues; the process of strengthening the economy of the country is also one of its most important aspects.

Economic diplomacy is not merely concerned with negotiations of commercial issues; the process of strengthening the economy of the country is also one of its most important aspects. This issue is particularly relevant to developing countries, but developed economies also go through a continuing development process. In other words, economic diplomacy at a bi-lateral level should be a continuing phenomenon; in this process proposals for infrastructural development, private foreign investments, capacity building, etc. must also be negotiated. Dynamism in ideas should be the driving force behind economic diplomacy.

Economic diplomacy is based on the capacity of parties to create opportunities and in this process the status of the parties should not assume much importance for it is an exercise which is based on creativity. A developing country's diplomat can be as creative; indeed, many of them are. The product of creativity may be progressively achieved through "capacity building".

One of the basic differences between economic diplomacy and the "mainstream diplomacy" is that whereas the latter is primarily concerned with developing and maintaining inter-State relationships, economic diplomacy is a more specific form of diplomacy with specific objectives like those of applied sciences—whatever may be agreed upon through economic diplomacy should be implemented in a tangible form—industry or anything that will add to the development process, in the State. Economic diplomacy is concerned with reality based on a country's capacity—intellectual, industrial, scientific, etc.

Creativity in relation to the best utilisation of the reserves of a country—human and natural—is one of the important objectives of economic diplomacy at an inter-State level. Economic diplomacy is not solely concerned with gaining economic or commercial benefits for others; one of its principal objectives is to create and maintain rapport with other countries.

Like mainstream diplomacy, economic diplomacy is to be operated as a vehicle to reach a predetermined destination, which is the creation and maintenance of bi-lateral commercial relationship for mutual interest. The term "mutual interest" should not be misconceived. "Interest" in this context would mean economic and commercial interest,[3] of both the sending and receiving States. The term "mutual" in this context would mean "performed by each of the parties concerned towards or with regard to the other(s); reciprocal."[4] This meaning is relevant when both the parties to an agreement are of similar standing, economically, commercially or otherwise; but when the parties are not so, "mutuality of interest" would not be achieved, and in that situation, the lesser party should not take a subservient role but try to negotiate businesses in a way whereby both parties would benefit, for example, a developing country, instead of looking for an opportunity to import foreign products, should propose a BOT (Build, Operate and Transfer) programme with that country whereby the richer country would set up the industry in the lesser (developing country) and train indigenous people so that eventually they are able to manufacture the product and export to that country on mutually beneficial terms. The lesser country will have to import that product only for a short period of time. There is always room for well thought-out strategies. It is important to ensure that in the name of diplomacy countries are not engaged in what may be described as "diplomacy of dependency".

Economic diplomacy should progress through stages: Short-term, medium-term and long-term. Whereas short-term diplomacy (which should not exceed a period of five years) is to be engaged for achieving short-term objectives, namely, import contracts or contracts for any other short-term objectives on a reciprocal or concessional arrangement. The subject matter of medium-term diplomacy would be such which would aim at capacity building in collaboration with a foreign partner a successful negotiation of which would lead to a bi-lateral investment treaty between the two countries, on the basis of which commercial contracts, including investment contracts which usually take the form of State contracts would be concluded. One of the important aspects of

[3] "Mutual scientific interest" should not really be included in economic and commercial interest.

[4] *The New Shorter Oxford English Dictionary*, Oxford, Clarendon Press (1993) at 1869.

long term economic diplomacy is to ensure that indigenous production by indigenous means is achieved in order to lessen dependency on others. The link between a medium-term and long-term diplomacy is obvious in that whereas medium-term diplomacy will lead to long-term diplomacy and the latter should provide economic self-sufficiency. During the medium term, for example BOT (Build, Operate and Transfer) schemes, which have already been explained, should be negotiated. BOT schemes have already been discussed in this chapter.

It has already been stated that in the contemporary period, economic diplomacy is required to be done at three levels—national, regional and truly international, the latter primarily for framework policies and regulations, and this issue has received further attention in a separate chapter of this work.

Based on the above discussion, it is reiterated that the primary aim of economic diplomacy at a national level is to achieve national self-sufficiency and expertise to become competitive in the world markets. This also must be achieved through reciprocal arrangements bearing in mind that economic diplomacy is the main vehicle for developing other forms of rapport with other States. But a successful economic diplomacy alone cannot make a country self-sufficient; an effective democratic political system guaranteeing the rights and freedoms of people with an unbiased judicial system is a sine qua non to achieving a sustainable and lasting economic diplomacy. It is important to build confidence in the minds of foreign investors by developing appropriate protective legislation and operating a reliable judiciary.

Economic diplomacy is not meant for developing business relationships with others but also for strengthening the country's infrastructure and intellectual capacity. A good economy is that economy which is knowledge-based. It becomes a source of creativity. Economic diplomacy need not be solely developed between a developed and a developing country; it should be developed between a developed and a developed country; and developing and developing too. There can be a variety of sources of mutual benefits, and these benefits need not necessarily take the forms of financial aid or transfer of technology. Exchange of ideas even between countries of similar economic standings can prove useful.

It has already been explained that economic diplomacy should be compared with a vehicle for a purpose. Its driving force is the idea that a diplomat must provide; but this vehicle should be driven continuously and with a moderate speed, as otherwise, any high-speed negotiation of issues may not lead to a meaningful and lasting business relationship with the other party.

Economic diplomacy shapes foreign policy-making of a country, that is, the commercial importance of a country is borne in mind by a country in developing her foreign policy vis-à-vis that country. Thus, an important aspect of economic diplomacy is to become competitive in all senses of the term so as to ensure that mutual benefits in their real terms are enjoyed by both the parties.

The caution must be entered however that if the political relationship between two countries is strained, the foundation of economic diplomacy with that country will be sapped; the interrelationship between the two types of diplomacy is close, and therefore should be maintained intact, if not at all impossible.

The nexus between economic diplomacy and a stable political regime is direct; in fact, all good private foreign investors and governments would prefer the existence of a stable political regime that recognises the rights and freedoms of people to any other form of regime. Predictability and certainty of governmental policies are important for strengthening economic ties with other States.

CHAPTER 2

The Focus of Economic Diplomacy Foreign Policy-Making

2.1 Introduction

The objectives of economic diplomacy have already been considered. Economic diplomacy at a bi-lateral level with a view to strengthening and enriching the national socio-economic infrastructure, growth and development has a relatively narrow scope but by no means a less significant activity. Economic diplomacy at a national level may benefit only the two countries which engage themselves for realistic reciprocal arrangements with a view to achieving mutual benefit. As stated earlier, such bi-lateral arrangements often lead to meaningful foreign relations too.

The plans, strategies and objectives of economic diplomacy at an international level are very different from those at a bi-lateral level. The primary objectives of such diplomacy are to identify specific issues which deserve the serious attention of the international community and formulate principles and policies for their implementation at national levels. The scope of this type of diplomacy is much broader than that at national level, and the competence of participants in this form of diplomacy should be unchallengeable. They must be well-informed of the issues and matters and clear of their goals. This is where "bargaining power"—the power to negotiate with logic and articulation matters.

In this chapter an attempt is made to identify and justify the kind of issues which deserve the attention of economic diplomacy at an international level, primarily at international fora. In fact, such issues and matters have already been identified in three very important documents, among

C. Chatterjee, *Economic Diplomacy and Foreign Policy-making*,
https://doi.org/10.1007/978-3-030-49047-8_2

others, namely, the Charter of Economic Rights and Duties of States 1974, the Doha Declarations of 2001 and 2005. These documents are now examined and analysed.

2.2 A Brief Examination and Analysis of the Documents

2.2.1 The Charter of Economic Rights and Duties of States, 1974[1]

The word "charter" signifies that it would provide certain principles and standards particularly relating to socio-economic issues which are vitally important for any country.

The timing of the Charter of Economic Rights and Duties of States (henceforth, the Charter) was interesting—the 1970s marked the beginning of the end of the decolonisation period. The newly born states perceived a new kind of socio-economic order, and their aspirations were translated into two documents in 1970—the New International Economic Order[2] and the Charter, but not all of these could be materialised.

One fundamentally important element of a successful diplomatic negotiation is not to approach any issue from a radical standpoint—every issue will have more than one dimensions, and it should be borne in mind that adherence to an issue rigidly in disregard of the others' viewpoints will not lead to any solution. Furthermore, no extremist views on any issue or matter will work in the world of diplomacy or for formulating international principles. This statement may be justified by referring to certain of the provisions of the Charter. Article 2, paragraph (c) of the Charter provides, inter alia, that:

> To nationalise, expropriate or transfer ownership of foreign property, in which case appropriate compensation should be paid by the State adopting such measures...

[1] UN General Assembly Resolution 3281(XXIX) of 1974; see also S K Chatterjee, "The Charter of Economic Rights and Duties of States: An Evaluation After Fifteen Years", 40 *International and Comparative Law Quarterly* (1991) 669–684.

[2] UNGA Resolution 3202(S-VI) of 16 May 1974 reproduced in 13 *International Legal Materials* (1974) 715.

Under customary international law, it is obligatory for sovereign states to pay prompt, appropriate and effective compensation in the event of their taking/nationalising/expropriating ownership in foreign property.[3] Such a provision would not receive the approval of the international community. In fact, this rule of customary international law would protect the interests of both developed and developing countries.

Articles 5 and 6 of the Charter promote what may be described as "Cartelisation" of commodities, trade, which is contrary to the principles of competition. Article 6, in particular, provides, inter alia, that:

> It is the duty of States to contribute to the development of international trade of goods, particularly by means of arrangements and by the conclusion of long-term multilateral commodity arrangements, where appropriate, and taking into account the interests of producers and consumers.

Care must be taken to ensure that in the name of economic diplomacy, economic conflicts are not created. Any attempt to satisfy certain narrow interests will not succeed at an international level. Common interests of the international community have to be identified so that they form the platform for any work plan.

On the other hand, the inclusion of "apartheid", "racial discrimination", "neo-colonial", etc. in Article 16 did not receive support from all the developed worlds' delegates at the conference which considered this instrument. They also found the latter part of this Article unacceptable. The full text of paragraph 1 of this Article is reproduced below:

> It is the right and duty of all States, individually and collectively, to eliminate colonialism, apartheid, racial discrimination, neo-colonialism and all forms of foreign aggression, occupation and domination, and the economic and social consequences thereof, as a prerequisite for development. States which practise such coercive policies are economically responsible to the countries, territories and peoples affected for the restitution and full compensation for the exploitation and depletion of, and damages to, the

[3] In this context, see UN GA Resolution 1803 (XVII) of December 1962; Awards of Arbitral Tribunals, for example, in *Libyan-American Oil Co* and Libya, 62 *International Law Reports* at 220; *Texaco and Calasiatic Co v Libya* 17 *International Legal Materials* (1978) 1.

> natural and all other resources of those countries, territories and peoples. It is the duty of all States to extend assistance to them.

This provision may not seem to be very relevant to the theme of the Resolution, but perhaps the developing countries decided to let their emotion out based on their experience in colonialism; on the other hand, apartheid, until the new South Africa was created, remained integrated into the economy. Perhaps, this should not be regarded as a damaging provision of the Charter. Developing countries did not wish to witness a repeat of the history as a precautionary measure.

Otherwise, the Charter correctly identified the socio-economic issues to which economic diplomacy should pay particular attention. At this point, it would be appropriate to examine the basic provisions of the Charter from the standpoint of economic diplomacy.

The Preamble to the Charter embodied the aspirations of the drafters for the creation of conditions for a number of issues, which were, in the main:

a. the attainment of wider prosperity among all countries and of higher standards of living for all peoples;
b. the promotion by the entire international community of economic and social progress of all countries, especially developing countries.

These aspirations may not be materialised unless every individual is allowed free access to education up to a certain level. A high level of public awareness is a sine qua non of socio-economic progress too. As stated earlier, economic diplomacy embraces almost all aspects of socio-economic issues; it is essential that economic diplomacy is directed at transboundary education without any barriers, whereby all States would be required to transmit knowledge to the less knowledgeable as part of a capacity building process.

The Charter advocated socio-economic development by participatory means—the promotion by the entire international community—whereby every participant would have mutual advantage and equitable benefits in the economic, trade, scientific and technical fields. Bridging the economic gap between developed and developing countries was one of the most important "concerns" of the Charter, and indeed, this should also be one of the primary themes of economic diplomacy. The Charter therefore advocated dismantling of the main obstacles in the way of the economic development of the developing countries. It is also noteworthy that the Charter emphasised the importance of the protection, preservation and enhancement of the environment as an essential element of socio-economic development.

The broader aspect of economic diplomacy should be concerned with the establishment and maintenance of a just and economic and social order, and to this effect, the Charter very clearly identified the goals of international economic diplomacy:

- the achievement of more rationale and equitable international economic relations and the encouragement of structural changes in the world economy;
- the creation of conditions which permit the further expansion of trade and intensification of economic co-operation among all nations;
- the strengthening of the economic independence of developing countries; and
- the establishment and promotion of international economic relations, taking into account the agreed differences in development of the developing countries and their specific needs.[4]

The fundamentals of international economic diplomacy may also be extracted from the Fundamentals of International Economic Relations identified by the Charter:

- Sovereignty, territorial integrity and political independence of States;
- Sovereign equality of States;
- Non-aggression;
- Non-intervention;
- Mutual and equal benefit;
- Fulfilment in good faith of international obligations;
- Respect for human rights and fundamental freedoms;
- No attempt to seek hegemony and spheres of influence;
- Promotion of international social justice;
- International co-operation for development; and
- Free access to and from the sea by land-locked countries.

That international economic diplomacy should not be a "diplomacy of domination", the Charter emphasises by providing the following:

[4] See the Preamble to the Charter.

> Every State has the sovereign and inalienable right to choose its economic system as well as its political, social and cultural systems in accordance with the will of its people, without outside influence, coercion or threat in any form whatsoever.[5]

Furthermore, any interference in the domestic affairs of a State by another State or coercion or threat to a foreign sovereign State runs counter to Article 2, paragraph 4 of the UN Charter; it will amount to "use of force" by a Member of the United Nations against another Member of it. Examples of such interferences exist (North Vietnam or Nicaragua or Yugoslavia or Iraq) but no effective diplomatic efforts were made by the international community to prevent the external powers from intervening into the domestic affairs of these countries either because they lent their tacit support to such interventions or they failed in their efforts. Political or military interference in the domestic affairs of another State will have a very significant and long-term effect on economic relations at a bi-lateral or even at a multilateral level. These acts may also give rise to polarisation of States which should be avoided by all means.

By the same token in Article 2, paragraph 2(b), the Charter provides that:

> Transnational corporations shall not intervene in the internal affairs of a host State.

Thus, the Charter implicitly recommended that host States should have appropriate laws and regulations to regulate and supervise the activities of transnational corporations within their national jurisdictions and to ensure that their activities conform to their (host States') economic and social policies.[6]

Economic diplomacy at a bilateral level should be directed at negotiations whereby development may be achieved by indigenous means through the participation of the country's own people. It is for each State to choose its goals of development, fully to mobilise and use its resources—both national and human. This has also been stated in Article

[5] Article 1 of the Charter.

[6] Article 2, paragraph 2(b).

7 of the Charter. Economic diplomacy must thus be based on a country's goals and available resources; there is no need to follow any model because one size may not fit all.

Initially, it may be difficult to achieve this goal solely through a country's own efforts. Thus, in so far as development of the industry sector is concerned, as stated before that BOT (Build, Operate and Transfer) method might be useful. Rational and equitable international economic relations in order to achieve structural changes[7] in economies should be another goal of economic diplomacy.

As stated earlier, one of the aims of economic diplomacy at an international level is to form and strengthen the platform of international co-operation in the economic, social, cultural, scientific and technological fields for the promotion of economic and social progress throughout the world, especially that of the developing countries.[8]

Diplomats are required to respond to the changing needs of international economic co-operation, and in order to achieve this objective, they are required to effectively participate in the international decision-making process, that is, principally, through the appropriate international organisations.[9] Much work has yet to be done on this issue—whether participation of the Member States should be based on quantum of their subscriptions or as groups of States. It must be pointed out however that participation of the Member States of the UN on various UN organisations does not necessarily depend on quantum of their subscriptions; their role in the world economy expressed or represented through their activities at the national and international levels. Usually, membership on committees rotate whereby each State is given an opportunity to participate in them. This does signify that in order to effectively participate in international organisations, diplomats, as delegates of their countries should have the capacity and ingenuity to persuade others with their objectives at international fora. Herein lie the essential qualities that a successful diplomat should possess and demonstrate to others to make them consider his/her points.

[7] Article 8 of the Charter.

[8] Article 9 of the Charter.

[9] See Article 10 of the Charter.

Article 14 of the Charter is concerned with the issue of increasing expansion and liberalisation of trade which should lead to the improvement in the welfare and living standards of all peoples. Thus, it provides, inter alia, that:

> Accordingly, all States should co-operate, inter alia, towards the progressive dismantling of obstacles to trade[10] and the improvement of the international framework for the conduct of world trade, and, to these ends, co-ordinated efforts shall be made to solve in an equitable way the trade problems of all countries, taking into account the specific trade problems of the developing countries.

The purpose of dismantling obstacles to trade is to allow access to markets for all provided of course their goods and services are competitive in price and quality. But, the provisions of Articles 12 and 14 effectively contradict the idea of free market access.

Article 4 of the Charter provides, inter alia, that:

> In the pursuit of international trade and other forms of economic co-operation, every State is free to choose the forms of organisation of its foreign economic relations and to enter into bilateral and multi-lateral arrangements consistent with its international obligations and with the needs of international economic co-operation.

This is in conformity with a sovereign State's right to join any form of organisation for the purposes of enhancing its foreign economic relations, and for that purpose to be engaged in bilateral and multilateral arrangements which would be consistent with its international obligations. However, the terms and conditions of the membership of these organisations should not be so privileged compared to those of the others which would amount to monopolising membership of these organisations. In other words, the privileges accorded by one such organisation should not be radically or significantly different from that of the other similar organisations. This is where much diplomatic activity is required. The choice of an organisation may be based on historical or political affinity of States, but the economic advantages or privileges should

[10] Emphasis added.

not be based on that as that will run counter to democratic and non-discriminatory principles of international economic co-operation, and also of the Principles enshrined in Charter of the United Nations.

Article 12 of the Charter provides, inter alia, that:

> (i) States have the right, in agreement with the parties concerned, to participate in sub-regional, regional and interregional co-operation in the pursuit of their economic and social development. All States engaged in such co-operation have the duty to ensure that the policies of those groupings to which they belong correspond to the provisions of the present Charter and are outward-looking, consistent with their international obligations and with the needs of international economic co-operation, and have full regard for the legitimate interests of third countries, especially developing countries.

These provisions in many ways contradict the provisions of Article 14 of the Charter. Of course, one might argue that Article 52 of the UN Charter provides for regional arrangements too. But, historically, military regional arrangements were initially conceived to launch offensives against the then Soviet Union, but of course, by virtue of dispensation granted under Article XXIV of the GATT (General Agreement on Tariffs and Trade) EEC was set up in 1950. Article 14 provides, inter alia, that:

> Every State has the duty to co-operate in promoting a steady and increasing expansion and liberalisation of world trade and an improvement in the welfare and living standards of all peoples, in particular those of developing countries. Accordingly, all States should co-operate, inter alia, towards the progressive dismantling of obstacles to trade and the improvement of the international framework for the conduct of world trade and, to these ends, co-ordinated efforts shall be made to solve in an equitable way the trade problems of all countries, taking into account the specific trade problems of the developing countries.

The issue remains whether regional trading arrangements, particularly those constituted of rich countries, raise barriers to trade for the outsiders rather than dismantling obstacles to trade. The best example would be the European Union (the European Economic Area) which primarily caters for its Member States; but of course, it also grants access to its Associate Members or non-members on a quota basis. Many of the non-member countries do not have any access for two main reasons: (a) that after trading with its Members and Associate Members, there hardly remains any market for the products from third countries; and (b) that market access may be denied on the grounds of products being sub-standards, that is, they fail to meet the required standards set by the EU authorities. This latter point deserves further attention. Standard setting is good, but those who are unable to meet these standards, "capacity building" projects become essential for them. Thus, it is through diplomatic efforts that arrangements for capacity building through BOT (Build, Operate and Transfer) should be made on a bilateral basis in order to gain access to markets in the developed world.

Without dismantling obstacles to trade, there cannot be any liberalisation of world trade. Regional economic integrations raise obstacles to trade to non-member countries. Regional economic integrations that raise obstacles to free trade represent an abuse of sovereignty; furthermore, they run counter to the policy of globalisation of trade. Such integrations may not allow free movement of capital and human resources which are the direct objectives of globalisation. Based on the EU trade pattern it may be maintained that regional economic integrations composed of developed States, widen the gap between the developed and developing countries. By virtue of the absence of economically strong leaders within any developing geographical region, regional integrations composed of developing countries may not be successful.[11]

There exist contradictions between the provisions of Article 12 and those of Article 13 of the Charter. This latter Article provides for the promotion of international scientific and technological co-operation and the transfer of technology:

> ... with proper regard for all legitimate interests including, inter alia, the rights and duties of holders, suppliers and recipients of technology. In particular, all States should facilitate the access of developing countries to the achievements of modern science and technology, the transfer of technology and the creation of indigenous technology for the benefit of the developing countries in forms and in accordance with procedures which are suited to their economies and their needs.

[11] See further S K Chatterjee, "Forty Years of International Action for Trade Liberalization", 23 *Journal of World Trade* (1989) 45.

In this connection, the recommendations of the UN Commission on Transnational Corporations are worth referring to[12]; it also recommended "acquisition" rather than "transfer" of technology, and the development of indigenous technology. Two issues deserve attention in this context: (a) the extent to which international scientific and technological co-operation has taken place between transnational corporations and developing countries, and what type(s) of technology is/are usually transferred to developing countries[13]; and (b) whether as recommended in Article 12 of the Charter and the policies of these groupings should correspond to the provisions of the present Charter and are "outward-looking, consistent with their international obligations and with the needs of international economic co-operation..." An effective economic diplomacy should seriously address these issues and concerns.

Paragraph (4) of Article 13 provides that:

> All States should co-operate in research with a view to evolving further internationally accepted guidelines or regulations for the transfer of technology, taking fully into account the interests of developing countries.

Such guidelines have only been developed by UNCTAD,[14] and the majority of States have failed to develop legislation based on these guidelines so as to ensure that private foreign investors were required to respect them.

Article 14 of the Charter further provides that:

> ... States shall take measures aimed at securing additional benefits for the international trade of developing countries so as to achieve a substantial increase in their foreign exchange earnings, the diversification of their exports, the acceleration of the rate of growth of their trade, taking into account their development needs, an improvement in the possibilities for these countries to participate in the expansion of world trade, and a balance more favourable to developing countries in the sharing of the advantages resulting from this expansion...

[12] *Transnational Corporations in World Development*, UN, New York (1983) at 385.
[13] See further UNCTAD Draft Code of Conduct on Transfer of Technology (1985)
[14] Op. cit.

Interestingly enough, diversification of export trade has taken place between some of the Asian countries and the Middle East and Africa; diversification of export trade has not significantly happened between developing countries and developed countries. Thus, the fact remains that developing countries are still not, in general, capable of participating in the expansion of world trade. Most of the developing countries still make their foreign exchange earnings by exporting those products which they have been doing for a very considerable period of time. A few exceptions to this pattern should not nullify this assertion.

One can thus return to the already mentioned issue that the majority of the developing countries are still unable to meaningfully interact with developed countries owing to the lack of their expertise and technology-based knowledge. To a certain extent developing countries are also responsible for this situation—no concerted and effective diplomacy entailing enforcement of these recommendations has taken place, and that, they also have failed to effectively utilise their resources, both natural and human, in order to develop their indigenous technologies.

Indeed, Article 23 of the Charter provided that:

> To enhance the effective mobilisation of their own resources, the developing countries should strengthen their economic co-operation and expand their mutual trade so as to accelerate their economic and social development. All countries, especially developed countries, individually as well as through the competent international organisations of which they are members, should provide appropriate and effective support and co-operation.

There are two main issues in the above provision which merit consideration. First, as a measure for an effective mobilisation of their own resources, presumably, both human and natural, the developing countries should expand their mutual trade in order to accelerate their socio-economic development. In other words, economic diplomacy should be directed at equals too. Second, that all countries should utilise the expertise of the competent international organisations as members of those organisations. This is a clear message to players of economic diplomacy to utilise external expertise obviously with an understanding of the contributions that these organisations can make to accelerate the socio-economic development process in all countries, particularly, developing countries.

These two dimensions to economic diplomacy should be seriously considered by the players of economic diplomacy, that is, both the national economic institutions concerned, and the national diplomats.

It is important for developed countries to appreciate that so long as developing countries remain economically and technologically dependent on them, and remain poor, developed countries will suffer as they will not be able to profitably exploit those areas, which are, in many cases, very large markets. As a justification of this statement, only the trade and investment flow between developed countries need to be referred to. Article 17 of the Charter provides, inter alia, that:

> International co-operation for development is the shared goal and common duty of all States.

This is an important issue because as stated earlier, the concept of "development" is not uniquely associated with developing countries only. This is where effective collaborations between developed and developing countries proves to be essential. Developing countries can also work jointly with developed countries, for example, in matters of tourism or the protection of the environment or even in regard to educational development.

Article 18 was simply the outcome of the untiring efforts made by UNCTAD. The theme of this Article was to grant generalised system of preferences (GSP) to developing countries in respect of import–export trade. Under this system, developing countries' selected goods would be free from any duty when they may be exporting them to developed countries, but the goods entering into developing countries from developed countries would be subject to tariffs. The aim of this system is to encourage export from developing countries but to discourage importation of goods from developed countries. This proposal was put forward by UNCTAD at a time when WTO did not exist. GATT, in general, contested this proposal; indeed, in order to accommodate this proposal GATT had to be amended; but by virtue of the Unanimity rule under Article XXX of GATT, UNCTAD realised that the proposal would meet its death so to say. Thus, it had no other choice but to seek approval through an enabling clause.[15]

[15] See further S K Chatterjee, "Forty Years of International Action for Trade Liberalization", op. cit., at 58.

There are two main types of GSP—UN and EU, and the list of selected items/commodities that would be GSP-laid are chosen by the grantor States; GSPs are renewed on an annual basis in consequence of which there does not exist any certainty for the firms manufacturing GSP-laid products that may be able to sustain their existence. It is also to be noticed whether developing countries save for a few have any special expertise in producing/manufacturing certain products included in a GSP list.[16]

Article 18 provides, inter alia, that:

> Developed countries should extend, improve and enlarge the system of generalized non-reciprocal and non-discriminatory tariff preferences to the developing countries consistent with the relevant agreed conclusions and relevant decisions as adopted on this subject, in the framework of the competent international organizations. Developed countries should also give serious consideration to the adoption of other differential measures, in areas where this is feasible and appropriate and in ways which will provide special and more favourable treatment, in order to meet the trade and development needs of the developing countries.

By the same vein, Article 19 of the Charter was drafted. The generalised systems of preferences are an innovative idea adopted by UNCTAD, but developing countries, in general, should appreciate that concessions and aid give rise to economic dependency—thus; appropriate and effective domestic economic policies should be adopted and implemented by them.

Articles 22, 24 and 25, in particular, give developed countries special responsibilities in regard to the following:

a. promotion of increased net flows of real resources including financial resources to the developing countries;
b. avoidance of any act which would prejudice the interests of developing countries; and
c. focusing special attention to the particular needs and problems of the least developed countries, land-locked and island developing countries with a view to helping them to overcome their particular difficulties.[17]

[16] See further S K Chatterjee; op. cit.

[17] Article 25.

Article 26 recommended that:

> International trade should be conducted without prejudice to generalized non-discriminatory and non-reciprocal preferences in favour of developing countries, on the basis of mutual advantage, equitable benefits and the exchange of most-favoured-nation treatment.

Two points merit consideration in regard to this provision: (a) whether developed countries would be prepared to be engaged in trade with developing countries on the basis of non-reciprocal preferences for an indefinite period of time; and (b) whether MFN treatment necessarily creates equality between States.

The Charter however strikes to a certain extent a degree of balance on this point by addressing certain issues and giving certain special responsibilities to developing countries. These appear particularly in Articles 20, 21 and 23. In Article 20 the Charter recommended that developing countries should "... in their efforts to increase their overall trade, give due attention to the possibility of expanding their trade with socialist countries..." It is not certain whether all developing countries will respect this recommendation because many of them hold prejudice against socialist countries. But it reminds the developing countries that in expanding their trade into socialist countries they must grant these countries conditions for trade not inferior to those usually granted to developed countries.

Article 21 of the Charter rightly recommended developing countries to promote the expansion of their mutual trade, grant trade preferences to other developing countries provided "... these arrangements do not constitute an impediment to general trade liberalisation and expansion". This is a practical approach for three reasons: (a) that this will diminish dependency of developing countries on developed countries; (b) trade is the primary vehicle to creating friendship with other countries which would lead to dependable political relationship with these countries; and (c) for reasons already stated above, regional economic integrations in the developed world would gradually deny/restrict developing countries market access. Developing countries, in general, are not short of natural and human resources; it might be quite beneficial for them to strengthen their own position through indigenous means, although initially they may have to do what is known as "capacity building" with the help of the more advanced countries. Indeed, Article 23 is also based on similar premises. It provided, inter alia, that:

> To enhance the effective mobilisation of their own resources, the developing countries should strengthen their economic co-operation and expand their mutual trade so as to accelerate their economic and social development.

Development forms the bases for mutual "economic co-operation" is the main goal of economic diplomacy or for the mainstream diplomacy too. Non-mobilisation of human resources has become an almost common phenomenon in the developing world. Here, the issues of prioritisation and "capacity building" including technical training of human resources remain important.

It is interesting to note that the Charter not only referred to economic development, but also social development. In fact, without any extensive social development, economic development would be meaningless. It is therefore important that in pursuing economic diplomacy, the issue of social development is borne in mind as social development (capacity building, education, health) process must be an essential facet of economic development organised through economic diplomacy.

The Charter recommends the developed countries to pay particular attention to developing countries in regard to most of the issues which have been embodied in it. What is stated in Article 28 is acceptable, but the international community might take time to implement it in its fullest form, and perhaps, its total implementation will never take place. This Article provides that:

> All States have the duty to co-operate in achieving adjustments in the prices of exports of developing countries in relation to prices of their imports so as to promote just and equitable terms of trade for them, in a manner which is remunerative for producers and equitable for producers and consumers.

The Charter is one of the few documents which have included "Common Responsibilities towards the International Community". These common responsibilities primarily relate to resources of the seabed, ocean floor and the subsoil thereof, which were recognised as the "common heritage of mankind". According to the Charter, States shall ensure that:

> ... the exploration of the area and exploitation of its resources are carried out exclusively for peaceful purposes and that the benefits derived therefrom are shared equitably by all States...[18]

One of the most important provisions of this Charter has been embodied in Article 30. It provides, inter alia, that:

> The protection, preservation and enhancement of the environment for the present and future generations is the responsibility of the States. All States shall endeavour to establish their own environmental and developmental policies in conformity with such responsibility.

2.3 The Doha Development Round

This Round is also known as the Doha Development Agenda, which was a trade negotiation round of the World Trade Organization (WTO) and which commenced in November 2001. It was a Ministerial Declaration[19] which was adopted in Doha, Qatar, and such ministerial meetings took place in Cancún (Mexico) in 2003, Hong Kong in 2005, and related negotiations took place in Paris 2005, Potsdam (Germany) 2007 and in Geneva in 2004, 2006 and 2008. The principal objective of the Doha Round was to lower trade barriers internationally which would facilitate trade across national boundaries for all participants, in particular, developing countries.

This Declaration remains an important declaration as it identified, inter alia, the main issues with which socio-economic development in a country is concerned. This is the primary reason why people including diplomats who may be involved in trade and investment negotiations should be familiar with the contents of this Declaration.

Unfortunately, all the subsequent negotiations (post 2001) broke down in view of the fundamental differences in ideas between developed and developing States. Although the developing States, in general, do require protection for their agricultural and small industries sectors, they should not ignore the fact that some of the developed countries, namely, Australia, Canada, France, Japan, New Zealand, the UK and the United

[18] Article 29.

[19] The text of this Declaration has been in 41 *International Legal Materials* (2002) at 746.

States have also large agricultural sectors and that they would also like to maintain subsidies on agricultural products, among other products. This issue became evident in the Cancún Conference.[20] Negotiations could not therefore be proceeded with regard to industrial tariffs, non-tariff barriers, service and trade remedies, etc. In April 2011, the then Director-General of WTO, Mr Pascal Lamy asked the Members to reconsider the consequences of not implementing the Doha Ministerial Declaration of 2001.

In 2012, Mr Lamy further recommended a gradual considered work on the part of the Members to iron out the differences between the rich and poor States. This is where an effective diplomatic manoeuvre becomes relevant. On 7 December 2013, the Bali Ministerial Declaration successfully addressed the bureaucratic barriers to commerce, but as from January 2014 the future of the Doha Round of 2001 remains uncertain.

However, in order to establish that the differences between developed and developing countries still remain unbridgeable, it is worth pointing out briefly why each of the meetings subsequent to the first Doha failed to reach any agreement.

Cancún 2003 was intended to create a framework for further negotiations, but this Conference failed for several reasons: (a) the EU held a strong stance on certain issues to protect the interests of its Members, but the developing countries refused to consider them; (b) some of the participants failed to demonstrate any genuine interests in negotiating on any issue which would benefit the majority of the countries, for example, the US and the EU showed significantly different approaches to special and differential treatment; and (c) according to some of the delegates, the agenda of the Conference was too complex to decide on many issues included in it. Cancún clearly evidenced the fact that the North-South divide on subsidies on agricultural products, which incidentally is given a very broad definition, was very prominent. This is another important issue for diplomats engaged in economic diplomacy to resolve.

During the Geneva negotiations in 2004, the EU accepted the elimination of agricultural subsidies by a specific date. Developing countries felt very enthusiastic about the implementation of the EU's proposal for the

[20] See further C Chatterjee, "From Doha to Cancún: A Multilateral Trading System?" 54 *Amicus Curiae* (2004).

elimination of subsidies on agricultural products. But, again, the agreement was abandoned and set December 2005 as the date for the 6th Ministerial Conference to be held in Hong Kong.

However, prior to holding the Hong Kong Conference, trade negotiators decided to hold a session of negotiations in Paris in May 2005. At the Paris Session, France opposed any cut on subsidies to farmers, while Australia, Brazil, India, the EU and the United States failed to agree on issues relating to beef, chicken and rice.

At the Hong Kong Conference of 2005, nothing of any significant importance took place other than the deal reached by the trade ministers of most of the governments present there whereby the deadline for eliminating subsidies on agricultural products by 2013 was set. In view of the number of other outstanding issues being left unresolved, the Conference deferred the expected completion of the Round until the end of 2006, that is, the year in which Geneva Conference would take place.

The Geneva talks of 2006 also failed to reach an agreement on reducing subsidies on agriculture products and lowering import taxes. Of course, the US Trade Act 2002 which gave the President a broad trade authority was due to expire in 2007 and as then President, George W Bush's term would come to an end, it would be futile to discuss any amendments to the Act which must be approved by the Congress under a new regime.

Unfortunately, the negotiations at Potsdam in 2007 also broke down in view of the major disagreement between the United States, the EU, Brazil and India over opening up new markets in agricultural and industrial products in various countries and the old issue of reducing farm subsidies.[21]

Then came the Geneva Talks in 2008 on the Doha Round, but it failed to reach any agreement on the proposal that the developing States would receive special and differential treatment on safeguard measures. There were disagreements on issues, namely, special protection for Chinese and Indian farmers and African and Caribbean banana imports to the EU.[22] The negotiations came to an end over issues of agricultural trade between China, India and the United States.

[21] See D Palmer and L MacInnes, "G4 Talks Collapse, Throw Trade Round into Doubt", *Reuters*, 21 June 2007.

[22] See further A Beattie, "US Says China and India put Trade Talks in Jeopardy", *The Financial Times*, 28 July 2008.

In their declaration the G-20 Summit of World Leaders in London in 2009, pledged to complete the Doha Round. In 2010, Mr Pascal Lamy urged the US President, Mr Obama to end the trade disputes between Brazil and the United States over cotton subsidies, but he also highlighted the difficulty of obtaining agreement for the United States without the presidential fast-track authority and biennial elections. However, at the World Economic Forum in Davos in 2011, Mr D Cameron, the then British Prime Minister, requested the Forum to conclude Doha Talks by the end of the year.

In December 2013, under the leadership of the new Director-General, Roberto Azevêdo, negotiations of the Ninth Ministerial Conference were held in Nusa Dua, Bali, Indonesia and produced an agreement which was known as the "Bali Package" which focused on trade facilitation by lowering cross-border tariffs and other regulations which hinder international trade; and it was believed that the Bali Package, if implemented in full, would significantly boost the global economy. This Package prescribed a 12-month deadline for the development of a clearly defined work programme.

The reasons for elaborating on the Doha Conferences and negotiations thereat are primarily twofold: (a) that negotiators (usually diplomats or other high-ranking government officials) must acknowledge the aspirations of both or all the parties concerned; and (b) that they must also have the skills to iron out their differences by sensible negotiations rather than rigidly adhering to their own ideas. Doha negotiations simply indicated that in the event of not paying attention to the above-mentioned issues attempts at negotiations may be made but no success may be achieved.

2.4 A Brief Examination of the Doha Ministerial Declaration, 2001

Since its establishment in 1945, the UN and its various Specialised Agencies have been consistently recommending the ways and means of achieving socio-economic development in the developing world, but the progress and examples of development have not been very evident for a variety of reasons, a discussion of which would go beyond the remit of this work. Suffice to say that academics belonging to various disciplines, namely, Economics, Sociology, Law, Geography, History, etc. have put forward various theories of "development" without providing a precise definition of the term. It has to be submitted however that, in reality, it would be very difficult to provide a precise definition of "development"; it may at most be described.[23] But development must be achieved through indigenous efforts with some guidance from experts, internal and/or external, but each country's development must be achieved according to the country's needs and strengths, including strengths derived from her human resources.

As from the 1970s developing countries have demonstrated their determination to achieve socio-economic development; indeed, that determination culminated in various instruments, namely, the Charter of Economic Rights and Duties of States, 1974, the Stockholm Declaration on the Protection of the Environment in 1972 and the Rio Declaration, 1992 among other such instruments, the provisions of which, are in fact, very relevant to socio-economic development. The essential factors of development are infrastructural development, including health, transport and communication, education, domestic industries, agriculture, etc. The Doha Ministerial Declaration of 2001 seems to have included in it most of the important essentials of socio-economic development. The primary headings under which this Declaration has been developed are the following: agriculture, services, trade-related aspects of intellectual property rights, relationship between trade and investment, trade facilitation, trade and environment, trade, debt and finance, trade and transfer of technology, technical cooperation and capacity building. Each of these items is extremely relevant to a socio-economic development process in any economy. In this context, it would be apposite to reproduce a part of the Declaration incorporated into its Preamble:

> We are determined ... to maintain the process of reform and liberalisation of trade policies, thus ensuring that the system plays its full part in promoting ... growth and development.

Another landmark step was taken by another Doha Declaration on Financing for Development, 2008.[24] A detailed discussion of the provisions of this Declaration would be beyond the remit of this work.

[23] See further S K Chatterjee, "International Law of Development" in *Encyclopedia of Public International Law*, Max Planck Institute for Comparative Public Law and International Law (1986).

[24] The text of this Declaration was published by the United Nations Department of Economic and Social Affairs, Financing for Development Office.

Nevertheless, it would be relevant to emphasise the interconnection between finance, trade and development which should include capacity building. This Declaration was primarily concerned with financing for development, and yet it referred to certain important issues, namely, development of human resources as human capital which is crucially essential for socio-economic development in any country. Furthermore, in most of the developing countries, domestic financial resources are not mobilised, thus they remain idle. This Declaration correctly identifies the need for mobilising financial resources for development "to provide universal access to basic economic and social infrastructures and inclusive social services, as well as capacity building..."[25] The Declaration of 2008 primarily contains a number of recommendations and future plans in regard to development, but they are very relevant to economic diplomacy. Paragraph 17 of the Declaration provided, inter alia, that:

> The development of a sound and broad-based financial sector is central to the mobilisation of domestic financial resources and should be an important component of national development strategies.[26]

This Declaration further recognises the importance of private international capital flows, particularly foreign direct investment as vital compliments to national and international development efforts. However, developing countries should, without any further delay, develop their foreign investment policies in a very articulate fashion, and pay their urgent attention to improving their judiciaries, where necessary, in order to develop confidence in the minds of private foreign investors.

In paragraph 36, the Declaration stated, inter alia, that:

> Aid for Trade is an important component of the measures that will assist developing countries in taking advantage of the opportunities offered by the international trading system, the outcome of the Doha round and regional trading agreements. A critical aim of Aid for Trade should enhance trade capacity and international competitiveness...[27]

[25] Op. cit., paragraph 13, at 8.

[26] Op. cit., at 9.

[27] Op. cit., at 16.

Based on historical evidence, it is emphasised that Aid for Trade should only be welcome in the capacity building of peoples with the provision of "buy-back", otherwise, the process will simply develop a high degree of what may be described as an "economy of dependence". But the Declaration rightly promotes the idea of South–South trade; an active implementation of this type of regional trade will create a wealth of knowledge, capacity building and friendly relations between the participants in the process. In addition to such a process, bi-lateral trading arrangements with rich countries will simply be profitable for both the parties particularly from the standpoint of monetary gains and capacity building and friendly relations.

In so far as the financing of trade, both domestic and export are concerned, governments should compulsorily develop and operate micro-financing system. This system will also strengthen the domestic world of finance.

The Doha Declaration on Financing for Development, 2008 identifies the areas of activity that need an urgent attention not only of domestic communities but also the international community.

2.5 Conclusions

As stated earlier, the Charter of Economic Rights and Duties of States was drafted at a time when most of the colonies attained their independence. In many ways, the Charter expressed the objectives of developing countries some of which are sustainable, others are mere aspirational. On the other hand, it was a timely movement to alert the world business community that the contemporary business attitudes and practices were not entirely satisfactory.

Although the diplomatic efforts in developing such a document with a significant contribution from developing countries were laudable particularly during a period when the tension between the developed and developing countries was quite transparent, a balanced view to keep the developed countries happy would have been better. This is an important point for striking profitable deals through economic diplomacy. Negotiations must be progressive and gradual; any drastic efforts to change a long-drawn practice, irrespective of whether it is entirely sustainable or not, will not succeed. Despite a number of constructive suggestions made through this Charter, owing to certain of the rather drastic views incorporated in it, it failed. But nevertheless, it identified some of the most important issues with which economic diplomacy should be concerned. It should also serve as a document that created "awareness" for the world business community of what were the contemporary deficiencies in the world of trade and investment.

CHAPTER 3

The Tenets of Economic Diplomacy and Foreign Policy-Making

3.1 Introduction

In this chapter, an attempt is made to examine the nature of the so-called "bargaining power" of the parties that are thought to play an active role in achieving objectives through economic diplomacy. Economic diplomacy of dependency has become an age-old phenomenon; and there are two reasons for it: (a) the psychological effect of colonialism the prevalence of which still seems to be manifest; and (b) developing countries, in general, seem to carry with them a degree of diffidence rather than confidence at negotiation tables. Both reasons need to be reviewed, and both are correctable. Whereas the former has its origin in the long process of domination of one by the other, including the former's thinking process; (b) the latter seems to be a direct consequence of the former.

Economic diplomacy is very much concerned with policy-making between States and also with the international community. In fact, it should really be a "participatory diplomacy" when diplomats assemble at international fora for framework policies and regulations. The prerequisites for "participatory diplomacy", are, in the main: (a) informed participants; (b) a clear understanding of the issues and matters of international "concern"; (c) prepared for listening to others' strategies and (d) tolerant of each other's views. A narrow perspective of any issue or matter of international concern will have no room in such diplomacy. These prerequisites for a participatory diplomacy necessarily lead one to the thorny issue of selection method(s) of diplomats. It is appreciated that

C. Chatterjee, *Economic Diplomacy and Foreign Policy-making*,
https://doi.org/10.1007/978-3-030-49047-8_3

this is a matter which comes under the exclusive domain of a sovereign government, but in view of the growing complexity of issues and matters in the contemporary world, it is important to ensure that diplomats have knowledge and experience in a number of disciplines and that they go through training programmes periodically with a view to keeping themselves up to date with the contemporary issues, be they economic or politico-economic in nature.

The Vienna Convention on Diplomatic Relations, 1961 identifies, in general, the functions of diplomatic missions, but not of diplomats presumably on the assumption that they should know them, but whatever their duties might be, diplomats must have the faculty/expertise to "negotiate" issues and matters with others. This is particularly important for economic diplomacy, which requires, inter alia, the capacity/faculty to strike a balance of interests between parties at a bi-lateral (bi-lateral treaties) or a multilateral level. Indeed, the membership of the World Trade Organization (WTO) entails acceptance of at least two instruments: The Agreement Establishing the World Trade Organization and the Multilateral Trade Agreements because the principles developed by these Agreements must be accepted by all the Members of it. Diplomats engaged in economic diplomacy must have knowledge to negotiate such agreements too, rather than leaving them to lawyers.

Contrary to the popular belief, negotiations are not based on battles of "muscle power" which is popularly described as "bargaining power"—in fact, "bargaining power" means the power to negotiate; it is a brain-based power, and not a power based on a country's other strengths, military, economic or otherwise. If "bargaining power" were based on "muscle power" then there would be no need for "negotiation" because the conclusion would be predetermined. The power to negotiate issues/matters may not be inherited from anywhere; it is developed through conceptualisation of ideas, which would be translated into words, and expressed in an articulate fashion. A good negotiator must realise that all negotiations are a "two-way" process; in other words, they must perceive the other party's strategies and goals too. Most of all, the needs of the other party must also receive mutual recognition and consideration. The same approach should also be taken when matters or issues are discussed at an international level.

The reality of international economic diplomacy is that there is no easy "walk-over" for any party in negotiating any matter or issue in relation to economic matters; this is because if the economic bases of a country are not kept protected and secured then the country will effectively be economically dependent on others; hence the need for economic reciprocity between States. If the strength of an economy is not sustainable, areas of political economy of that country will be adversely affected.

The reality of general diplomacy is that the more economically strong a country is, the more recognised it would be from a political perspective too; the country's voice will be heard by the international community. The interrelationship between economic/commercial diplomacy and general diplomacy is quite close. Recently, despite its general abhorrence of the Russian action over Ukraine (Crimea) the government of the United Kingdom did not plan to cut-off its trade relationship with Russia; trade and commerce between States always offer platform for further rapport between them. It would be appropriate to maintain that economic/commercial diplomacy forms the basis for general diplomacy between States.

3.2 The Principal Tenets of Economic Diplomacy

The principal tenets of economic diplomacy may be derived from its objectives, which are to develop and maintain rapport between States based on trade, commerce and investments as well as to develop framework regulations for the international community in regard to the conduct of players engaged in economic/commercial diplomacy, and to promote policies in regard to matters of "international concern" bearing an economic/commercial dimension. Based on this theme, the tenets of economic diplomacy may be identified and discussed.

3.2.1 Reciprocity

One of the most important aspects of diplomacy, be it economic or otherwise, is to develop reciprocity between States based on "functional" sovereignty of a State. Indeed, it is important to appreciate that the concept of "sovereignty" is not to be understood and applied in its narrowest perspective when interacting with another sovereign State.[1] Application of sovereignty as a law-maker in the domestic sphere of a sovereign State, and its application for developing relations with foreign

[1] See further C Chatterjee, *International Law and Diplomacy*, London, Routledge (2007) at 47.

sovereigns should be different. It is elementary to mention that without any meaningful functional relationship with the wider community, a sovereign, no matter how strong it may be, will be totally isolated, and economically/commercially poor as without reciprocity with others, it would be unable to gain markets for its products or create opportunities for investments in foreign jurisdictions. Incidentally, in developing reciprocity, it is important to ensure that both the parties can exchange business deals between themselves. In developing reciprocity, developing countries should not take any defensive position or a position of dependency. Developing countries have potentials too, most often they are not utilised effectively, for a variety of reasons: the lack of policies, or the lack of opportunities primarily occasioned by domestic factors, which in many cases, may have to be appreciated. However, one is nevertheless required to move forward. There exist ways and means to overcome the cycle of economic/commercial stagnation. Take, for example, the BOT (Build, Operate and Transfer) or the BOOT (Build, Own, Operate and Transfer) schemes.

There also exists a very deep-seated perception that developing countries cannot reciprocate with developed countries as either they have nothing to offer to the latter or that they lack the required bargaining power; both the assumptions are unfounded. Reciprocal arrangements need not be made only in regard to providing goods and services; BOT or BOOT, for example, forms the foundation of reciprocity between developed and developing countries.

The misconception of "bargaining power" should be critically examined. "Bargaining power" means "the power to negotiate", which can be exercised by any individual endowed with wisdom. This cannot be a reserved domain of developed countries only. Military or economic might of a country should not be allowed to cloud a negotiation process, and if they are allowed to do so, then there is no need to initiate any negotiation process; the result would be predetermined. Diplomacy of force must be avoided.[2] However academic it might sound, over the past three decades, in particular, the international community seems to have preferred to apply or support military interventions which are contrary to the Charter of the United Nations (Article 2 paragraph 4) to which the vast majority of the States belong. This needs to be reviewed again

[2] See further C Chatterjee, *International Law and Diplomacy*, London, Routledge (2007) Paperback edition (2010) at 71–72.

by the international community by examining the nature of the results it has achieved. It is not by military might or economic coercion that reciprocity between States may be developed; friendship forms the foundation of peace, and economic diplomacy provides the platform for it. In order to justify this view, one may like to refer to the following among other examples—the Vietnam war, the intervention in Kuwait, the intervention in the former Yugoslavia, Afghanistan, Iraq, Libya to name but a few. What has the international community achieved by using military might? These regimes could have been changed by non-military means too.

3.2.2 A Meaningful Co-operation?

To "co-operate" means to "act together". "Togetherness" in this context does not mean merely to join the others together; it would mean "sharing of ideas" or "creating new ideas" as a club of States represented by their diplomats. The unity of minds as a basis for a common theme must be achieved first; however, it may not be effectively achieved unless each participant has a clear idea of the theme and that the members of the club have identified the policies and strategies of the opponents too. In other words, for a meaningful international co-operation, the similarities and differences in interests are to be clearly identified at the initial stage of international co-operation. In fact, this stage should be called a "preparatory" stage for a meaningful international co-operation. But, there may not be any meaningful co-operation unless parties are tolerant to each other.

In achieving any meaningful international co-operation between the representatives of States, the interests of developed, developing and least developed countries must be taken into account, otherwise the effort will result in a failure, and the consequences of it may be far-reaching. Take, for example, the case of the Cancún Conference which took place in 2003. One of the main issues at Cancún related to the protection of the textile industries in textile producing countries, which generally comes under the agricultural sector of an economy because this industry is, in effect, based on the production of cotton. In promoting their protectionist ideas, the developing countries, many of which are cotton-producing countries, failed to appreciate that quite a number of countries in the developed world are also cotton-producing countries (namely, Australia, Canada, New Zealand and the United States let alone some of the European countries) and that they would like to protect their national interests too in regard to cotton production and textile industries. Developing countries therefore encountered a formidable opposition from those of the developed countries which had direct interests in the textile industry and the former were not prepared with sustainable answers to their views.[3] One can easily draw the inference that in order to strike any deal which would be beneficial for both the parties, the issue of the "mutual interest" assumes paramountcy. Identification of "mutual interest" and to lead it to maturity for the purpose of working in concert, and that is the beginning of international co-operation. The road based on international co-operation can be "bumpy"—rough, but creative negotiating technique should "smoothen" it up. In other words, "international co-operation" entails a continuing effort on the part of the parties having a "mutual interest" / international interest. Examples of any successful treaties of international co-operation (namely, the Nuclear Non-Proliferation Treaty, 1968) and other than bi-lateral investment and co-operation treaties are very few.

The classic philosophy on which mutual co-operation should be based was clearly stated by the Permanent Court of International Justice in the *River Oder Commission Case* which entailed a question of sharing functional sovereignty between the Member States of the Commission rather than perceiving that the River Commission would assume the Member States' sovereignty. The Court stated, inter alia, that:

> … when consideration is given to the manner in which States have regarded the concrete situations arising out of the fact that a single waterway traverses or separates the territory of more than one State, and the possibility of fulfilling the requirements of justice and the considerations of utility which this fact places in relief, it is at once seen that a solution of the problem has been sought not in the idea of right of passage in favour of upstream States, but in that of a community of interest of riparian States. This community of interest in a navigable river becomes the basis of a common legal right, the essential features of which are the perfect equality of all riparian States in the users of the whole course of

[3] See further C Chatterjee, "From Doha to Cancún: A Multilateral Trading System?", 54 *Amicus Curiae* (2005).

> the river and the exclusion of any preferential privilege of any one riparian State in relation to the others.[4]

From a pragmatic point of view, it may be stated that in this boundaryless world, in regard to international issues, "community of interests" should be identified, and work together towards the end, rather than maintaining any rigid view of sovereignty. There are certain issues, namely, drug-trafficking, money-laundering, cybercrime, slave trade where international co-operation for eradication of these acts is not only essential but also overdue.

3.2.3 Resolution of Issues and Matters of "International Concern"

Economic diplomacy at an international level is primarily concerned with international policy-making in regard to important international economic issues and matters. Incidentally, an "issue" refers to a specific question, whereas a "matter" has a broader perspective, for example, the impact of human rights issues on economic diplomacy—a rather broad question.

The international community is often required to consider issues/matters of "international concern", such as the issue of oil pollution and its impact on the living sea resources or the question of slavery and slave trade or the wider matter of whether "drugs consumption" should be legalised or not. Each of these issues/matters must be lobbied at an international level, and in order to do so, a State or a group of States will have to initiate the proposal. In other words, there should be a united voice on the issues/matters before they are initiated. In initiating such a proposal, the strengths and weaknesses of it, the rationale for promoting the proposal, including the predictable oppositions, should be included in such proposals.

In this effort, the State-based barriers of all kinds and nature must be dismantled, as matters and issues of international concern cannot be limited to narrow ideas and ideologies. In other words, whether a matter or an issue is a matter or an issue of "international concern" must first be established. There are ways and means of recognising and establishing a matter or an issue as one of international concern. In the Nuclear Tests

[4] Case relating to the *Territorial Jurisdiction of the International Commission of the River Oder*, PCIJ, Series a (1929) at 27.

cases[5] in establishing the legal interest of Australia, the Memorial of the Government of Australia stated, inter alia, that the concern of the peoples and of the countries for the urgent elimination of the risks connected with experimental explosives then progressively developed.[6] It went on to state that:

> The greater level of activity in nuclear testing by the United Kingdom, the United States and the Soviet Union in 1957-58 provoked increasing world-wide concern at the effect of the fall-out. A petition signed by 9,000 scientists from 49 countries was presented on 13 January 1958 to the Secretary-General, urging that an international agreement to stop the testing of nuclear bombs be made now.[7]

The UN General Assembly was eventually requested by UN Scientific Committee on the Effects of Atomic Radiation to adopt on 4 November 1958 resolution 1252 (XII) urging an early agreement on the end of testing. This episode was sufficient to confirm that nuclear tests were matters of international concern. Thus, it is for the international community to determine what matters/issues would be matters/issues of international concern.

It has been stated earlier that sovereignty should not be used in its "absolute" form other than in matters which come under its exclusive jurisdiction[8]; it should be used in its "relative" form when acting with others. Here, all participants must act on an equal level; there is no "primus" inter pares. Each participant is required to comprehend the adverse effect of matters/issues not only in one country or two but to the entire world. Again, a "unity of ideas" must prevail to convince the international platform concerned (the UN or its relevant specialised agencies) that it should be an "agenda item" for a full discussion leading to a binding Convention, Declaration or Resolution, etc.

It is to be emphasised however in this context that a mere conclusion of any of the above-mentioned instruments would not do; the parties

[5] *ICJ Reports* (1978).

[6] *ICJ Reports*, op. cit., at 332.

[7] Ibid.

[8] In the contemporary period, there are many so-called matters which do not in reality come under the exclusive jurisdiction of a State, for example, anti-money laundering, drug-trafficking, slavery or slave-trade etc.

participating in the making of any of them should implement them at a national level rather than raising the irrelevant issue that none of these instruments are binding. Such a question is irrelevant simply because it is elementary that the UN is not a law-making body in the sense a national parliament is; the UN has no parliament of its own; it cannot have one—it has no territory, it has no "people" to govern; most of all it is not a sovereign entity. The UN can only make framework legislation, it is for its Member States to appreciate the reason for its passing a framework legislation and implement it at each nation-level; otherwise one shall precipitate the current unhelpful and misconceived idea that UN Conventions or other instruments it may adopt is not binding.[9]

Article 2(2) of the UN Charter provides that:

> All Members, in order to ensure to all of them the rights and benefits resulting from membership, shall fulfil in good faith the obligations assumed by them in accordance with the present Charter.

This "pledge" amounts to a contractual obligation save that in the event of a Member State failing to perform its obligations, whether in the form of non-implementation of a provision of a convention or a declaration or a resolution or to deny altogether the importance and effectiveness of these instruments, the UN has not been endowed with any power to take its Member States to task, unless it is a matter which comes under Chapters VI or VII of the Charter. But, what is expected of the Member States? That answer may clearly be found at least in three places in the UN Charter—The Preamble to the UN Charter, and Articles 1 and 2 of it.

Sovereigns or their representatives should appreciate that most of the matters/issues of international concern in the world are created by States themselves either directly or indirectly, and that they should through their own efforts resolve them, or as stated earlier, draw the attention of the UN in a "united voice" to seek resolution of the matter/issue. All artificial divides and barriers between peoples based on culture, religion, faith, sex, origins and political ideologies must be eliminated, otherwise the absence of "peace" currently a "matter of international concern" may not

[9] These are examples however to evidence the fact that the UNGA Resolutions can be binding: The Uniting for Peace Resolution, 1950 or Permanent Sovereignty over Natural Resources, 1962, to name but a few.

be achieved. This is not a philosophical solution to the problems that the contemporary world has been experiencing; this must be treated as a realistic approach to set the foundation of peace, as there are no other alternatives to it. Powerful States may waste their wealth on warfares, but it is elementary that their acts cause death, human miseries and poverty, and then UN help is sought in the name of "humanitarian help" which amounts to spending money on non-creative activities.

Based on the post-Second World War non-peaceful events (since 1945) one may maintain that the West won the Second World War but lost world peace; in other words, the War was won at the cost of world peace. The answer is not that the conduct of the post-Second World War peoples or States was unforeseeable or unpredictable, but whether the post-second World War diplomacy has been effective enough to meet the requirements for peace or whether the behaviour of certain States or groups of people, factions have been contributing to warfares and whether contemporary diplomacy has utilised the international forum (the UN) or any other forum effectively for founding the principles of peace and developing any Code of Conduct for the purpose. Peace cannot be achieved through warfares. Absence of world peace is a matter of international concern. To make peoples subject to miseries to which they do not usually contribute is a matter of international concern. Likewise, "intervention" by States on humanitarian grounds is a matter of "international concern".

Contemporary international diplomacy has failed at least in regard to two issues: (a) the lack of "unity of ideas", based on negativism; and (b) the diplomacy of dependency[10] or submissiveness, a return to a revised version of colonisation. International diplomacy is not about relations between States only; the beneficiaries of it are peoples. From this standpoint, the classical principles of international diplomacy must be reviewed, and "modernity" must be brought into it; the aspirations of peoples in States may not be disregarded.

The atrocities caused by dictatorial governments to make their peoples suffer by denying their fundamental rights and freedoms, such as the right to education, the right to work, the right to equal treatment for all peoples in respect of all matters, the right to assemble peacefully and the right to set up "action groups" for creating public awareness, to name

[10] See further C Chatterjee, *International Law and Diplomacy*, London, Routledge (2010) at 72.

but a few are the sine qua non to satisfy the requirements of good governance. When these fundamental rights are denied to people, the regimes concerned are primarily responsible for their own "de-stabilisation", and their insensitivity to their peoples' rights and freedoms must be regarded as a matter of "international concern"—the issue of tradition, faith etc. should not be used as a barrier to democracy, as it is not conditional upon anything. A united peoples' concern should be deemed as a matter of "international concern".

In this connection, it must be pointed out that the scope of "economic diplomacy" should not be limited to "economic relations between States" only; matters which are apparently "non-economic" in nature also come within its scope, namely, the denial of politico-economic rights to peoples,[11] the environment in the workplace; the protection of the environment; the issue of the minimum wages; discrimination between employees, etc. Thus, what may usually be perceived to be a matter of "domestic concern" should be construed as a matter of "international concern".

It has also been stated before that economic diplomacy forms the basis for inter-State diplomacy, often described as "political diplomacy". The function of economic diplomacy, inter alia, is to develop policies both at domestic and non-domestic levels to benefit national societies by providing facilities and opportunities for a fuller life for everybody. In order to be able to achieve this, a democratic form of government combined with opportunities for education and the creation of "public awareness" among other issues would be essential, which are also the essentials for becoming a developed economy.

Economic diplomacy thus has a socio-political dimension too. In fact, any form of economic diplomacy, inter-State, or truly international, ultimately contributes to the socio-economic development at a domestic level. National initiatives as to issues and matters would help diplomats "master" that issue/matter to promote it to the status of an issue or matter of "international concern". Economic diplomacy is thus concerned with both domestic and international issues. Take, for example, the issue of "apartheid" in South Africa. It was originally a domestic issue of South Africa; with the help of certain external/internal initiatives, mainly of an individual nature, such as that taken by Bishop Huddleston or Mahatma

[11] See the International Covenant on Civil and Political Rights, 1966.

Gandhi of India, it primarily remained as a South African matter, until of course, Nelson Mandela through his unceasing efforts to abolish apartheid in South Africa drew the attention of the international community. Of course, India, Zambia and Zimbabwe, in particular, in addition to certain other countries, lent their support to the idea that it was a matter of "international concern". Not only the political system was based on apartheid in South Africa, but her economy also became an "apartheid economy". One should not forget the contribution made by the World Council of Churches in Geneva and the UN[12] to the anti-apartheid movement in South Africa. Issues of such nature, again, such as child army, child abuse, illicit drug-trafficking, etc. can only be effectively dealt with if the entire international community co-operates and treat them as matters of international concern leading to binding international norms.

3.3 Development of Framework Law

The term "framework" means:

> A supporting structure around which something can be built; system of rules, ideas or beliefs that is used to plan or decide something or a legal framework for resolving disputes.[13]

The first two meanings of the term are particularly relevant to economic diplomacy because this is precisely what diplomats at an international forum should do—develop supporting structure around which something can be built or develop system of rules, ideas or beliefs which may be used to plan or decide something. Again, in order to achieve this, a true "international co-operation" among States with a "unity of ideas" would be essential.

[12] One of the reasons why The Charter of Economic Rights and Duties of States 1974 (Res 3281) was not accepted by many States was that in Article 16 it incorporated the issue of apartheid. This is not to suggest that the entire international community is supportive of apartheid, but that its members failed to see the link between apartheid and economic rights and duties of States. See some of the other UN Resolutions on this issue. See further, S K Chatterjee, "The Charter of Economic Rights and Duties of States; An Evaluation After 15 Years", 40 *International and Comparative Law Quarterly* 669 at 681; see further C Chatterjee, *International Law and Diplomacy*, op. cit., at 298–299.

[13] *Cambridge Advanced Learner's Dictionary*, 3rd edition, Cambridge, Cambridge University Press (2008) at 567.

A supporting structure in the form of a resolution or declaration should then be transformed into legislation and implemented at national levels. Again, the issue of the legally binding effect of their instruments should not be raised and the reasons for supporting this view have already been explained. On the other hand, it is heartening to mention that since the inception of the United Nations, so many of such instruments have been adopted but almost to no avail, which is primarily due to the perception of "sovereignty" that members of the international community, in general, maintain.

Examples of Framework legislation may be found in the "Documents referred to" at the end of this work, and it is never too late for the international community to adopt and implement them in the form of legislation or even Codes of Conduct at national levels. It would be opportune to highlight two particular framework instruments which are directly concerned with private foreign investments. The first would be the UN Code of Conduct on Transnational Corporations, (1984) and the second, the UNCTAD Draft Code of Conduct on Transfer of Technology (1985). Only the most fundamental parts of these Codes of Conduct are now examined.

3.3.1 The UN Code of Conduct on Transnational Corporations

One should not disregard this Code of Conduct on the grounds of its age; it is to be pointed out that this Code of Conduct which was drafted by the UN Committee on Transnational Corporations is still valid, and has not been superseded by any subsequent code of conduct in relation to this matter.[14]

During the 1960s and 1970s many economies were effectively controlled by transnational corporations; this domination could be described as a second version of economic colonialism. There were various reasons for allowing transnational corporations to dominate those economies[15] and in the context of this work, there is no need to examine those causes. After over four decades, it would still be worth its while to examine the basic ethos of this Code of Conduct, which was addressed

[14] With the end of the mandate of this Committee, no further codes of conduct on this matter has been developed by any other UN institution.

[15] See further R Vernon, *Sovereignty at Bay*, London, Pelican Press (1973).

to both developed and developing States in order to highlight how the activities of transnational corporations may be best utilised by home and host States. This Code was based on empirical studies, which allowed it to identify private foreign investors' practices prevalent in both developed and developing countries. This Code has been discussed in Chapter 12 of this work.

3.4 Conclusions

Academics may devise many other tenets of Economic Diplomacy. The basic theme of this chapter has been to establish that it is for diplomats to take the initiatives to develop tenets of economic diplomacy according to the demands of the day. The rigid view of sovereignty maintained by many sovereigns seems to be a great hindrance to applying the tenets of economic diplomacy. Furthermore, it is for the sovereign states to develop their willingness to co-operate with each other to deal with issues of "international concern".

CHAPTER 4

The Boundaries of Economic Diplomacy and Foreign Policy-Making

4.1 Introduction

It is interesting to note that there does not exist any published work which identified the functions of a diplomat engaged in economic diplomacy. There may be two possible reasons for this: (a) that there exists an assumption that the diplomats are familiar with their functions; and (b) that it might be inappropriate to limit their functions particularly in view of the very broad spectrum of their activities with which they are concerned. Whatever may be the correct reason for not having any guidelines of their functions, it might nevertheless be appropriate to develop certain essential guidelines for them. Over the years, the UN or its agencies have developed a number of documents[1] in the form of resolutions or scientific papers, which when read together give clear indications as to the functions of diplomats engaged in economic diplomacy. One of the Resolutions of the UN General Assembly that outlined many of the functions of diplomats engaged in economic diplomacy, directly or indirectly, is the Charter of Economic Rights and Duties of States, 1974.[2] Although this

[1] See for example, the UNGA Resolution entitled Permanent Sovereignty over Natural Resources, 1962; the discussion papers of the Uruguay Round; the UNCTAD Resolution 45(III) of 18 May 1972—Proceedings of the United Nations Conference on Trade and Development, Third Session, vol I, Report and Annexes; the Doha Declarations of 2001 and 2005.

[2] This Resolution was adopted on 12 December 1974 with 50 abstentions at the material time.

C. Chatterjee, *Economic Diplomacy and Foreign Policy-making*,
https://doi.org/10.1007/978-3-030-49047-8_4

Resolution was not accepted by a number of developed States for their own reasons which need not be examined in the context of this work, most of its themes are still valid for economic diplomacy. It is important to point out in this context that in its Resolution 3082 (XXVIII) of 6 December 1973, the UN General Assembly reaffirmed its conviction of "the urgent need to establish or improve norms of universal application for the development of international economic relations on a just and equitable basis",[3] and urged the Working Group of Governmental Representatives on the Charter of Economic Rights and Duties of States to complete as the first step in the codification and development of the matter.

By late 1973, the international community showed its determination to establish a new international economic order which was clearly demonstrated by the UNGA's resolutions 3201 (S-VI) and 3202 (S-VI) of 1 May 1974 which contained the Declaration and the Programme of Action on the Establishment of a New International Economic Order which also stressed the fact the Charter of Economic Rights and Duties of States "shall constitute an effective instrument towards the establishment of a new system of international economic relations based on equity, sovereign equality, and interdependence of the interests of developed and developing countries."[4]

The Charter of Economic Rights and Duties did not come into force, which may be described as a "missed opportunity" for the international community (the rejectable parts of it, if rejected, the other parts of it could have been perfectly operational) but, as stated earlier, it nevertheless outlined the modern dimensions to economic diplomacy. The phoenix can still rise from the ashes of the dead Charter. The next step forward towards a new type of economic diplomacy was taken by the Doha Declarations of 2001 and 2005.

In this chapter these three instruments have received attention as they are directly relevant to the objectives of economic diplomacy.

[3] See the Text of the Resolution 3281 (XXIX) of 12 December 1974.

[4] See the statements made before the Preamble to the Resolution.

4.2 The Charter of Economic Rights and Duties of States, 1974

A charter should be regarded as a document which provides a framework legislation, the principal purpose of which is to familiarise the Members of the United Nations with the aspirations of the international community, and to implement them at a national level.[5] It also operates as a Code of Conduct in relation to the subject matter(s) of the Charter. It is worth noting that this is one of the very few documents developed under the auspices of the United Nations which not only refers to rights but also certain duties of the States, Members of the United Nations. This document aimed to be as comprehensive and pervasive as possible.

This document emphasised the purposes of the United Nations, in particular, the maintenance of international peace and security. One is required to accept that the purpose of the United Nations may not be achieved through warfares, but primarily through friendly relations among States. Thus, diplomats are required to learn the skills for promoting friendly relations among States. International law is concerned with "States" and not "nations", but the latter has been referred to in this context presumably because within a federal State, several nations exist, and nations have in appropriate cases may exercise their right of self-determination. Again, it is through friendly relations and international co-operation that international problems in the economic and social fields may be resolved.

The issue of the new international economic order on which UNGA passed resolutions should be seriously reflected upon. The world economy may no longer be totally tied with the Bretton Woods System. Secondly, since the resolutions—3201 (S-VI) and 3202 (S-VI) were adopted by the UN General Assembly on 1 May 1974, the world's economic landscape has also changed particularly with the advent of the emerging markets—China, India and Nigeria.

The industrial growth in the emerging markets and their aspirations for participation in the traditionally rich markets have indeed changed the business strategies for both the rich and the emerging markets.

[5] Incidentally, the UN Charter contains both binding obligations (Article 2 or Chapters VI and VII) as well as recommendatory directions addressed to its Members.

Furthermore, the UN also has shown its determination for strengthening international co-operation for development. In the Preamble to the Charter it was stated that:

> ... it is a fundamental purpose of the present Charter to promote the establishment of the new international economic order, based on equity, sovereign equality, interdependence, common interest and co-operation among all States, irrespective of their economic and social systems.

The Charter also pointed out that the promotion of the economic and social progress of all countries, including developing countries, is to be achieved by the entire international community. The philosophy on which this Charter is based may be applied to both socio-economic development process in a country and economic diplomacy, because the latter should take a proactive role in the materialisation of that philosophy, which, incidentally, is based on practical issues, namely, higher standards of living for all people, the promotion by the entire international community of the economic and social progress of all countries; or

> The encouragement of co-operation, on the basis of mutual advantage and equitable benefits for all peace-loving States which are willing to carry out the provisions of the present Charter, in the economic, trade, scientific and technical fields, regardless of political, economic or social systems.[6]

The Charter also referred to the need to establish and maintain a just and equitable economic and social order through the "... achievement of more rational and equitable international economic relations and the encouragement of structural changes in the world economy".[7] and by creating conditions which would permit the further expansion of trade and intensification of economic co-operation among all States. This provides sufficient hints as to what economic diplomacy is all about. Of course, in respect almost all of the issues which the Charter identified a special reference was made to the needs of developing countries.

It is also worth mentioning that the Charter reminded us of the need for promoting collective economic security for development through the co-operation of the entire international community. The crucial term is

[6] See the Preamble to the Charter.

[7] Ibid.

"co operation" at an international level, the factors of which are not easy to understand. However, a discussion of the concept of "international cooperation" may be found in a separate section of this work.

The Charter very rightly pointed out that:

> ... the responsibility for the development of every country rests primarily upon itself[8] but the concomitant and effective international co-operation is an essential factor for the full achievement of its own development goals.

The Charter has also emphasised that there is an "urgent need to evolve a substantially improved system of international economic relations."[9] This identifies another dimension to economic diplomacy—it is an evolutionary discipline; the system of improving international economic relations can never be a static concept; it falls on diplomats to take an active role in the process of improving international economic relations.

The Charter identified the fundamentals of international economic relations, which are still valid; briefly, these are: sovereignty, territorial integrity, sovereign equality of States, non-aggression and non-intervention, peaceful co-existence, self-determination of peoples, peaceful settlement of disputes, remedying of injustices which are brought about by force, fulfilment in good faith of international obligations, respect for human rights and fundamental freedoms, promotion of international social justice, international co-operation for development and of course, the protection of the rights of land-locked States by allowing them free access to and from the sea which is essential for allowing them to participate in the arena of international trade and water-based transport system.

4.3 The Nature of Economic Rights and Duties of States

The Charter maintains that

> ... every State has the sovereign and inalienable right to choose its economic system as well as its political, social and cultural systems in accordance with the will of its people, without outside interference, coercion or threat in any form whatsoever.[10]

[8] Emphasis added.

[9] See the Preamble to the Charter.

[10] Article 1 of the Charter.

This provision, when analysed, refers to a number of issues which are directly relevant to economic diplomacy. It emphasises that the issue of external interference or coercion or threat of any form must be prevented. It is in accordance with the "will of its people" that every State must choose its political, social and cultural systems. This provision therefore suggests that the "will of its people" must be recognised in forming various systems in a State—therefore, in effect, a people-led State—a democracy.

This is a crucially important issue in that it is usually perceived that democratic governments' policies will have a democratic rationale, although this provision may provoke controversy. There is another very important dimension to the above-mentioned provision—that is, over any State's economic, political, social and cultural systems, interference by any external institution or State is impermissible, unless of course, these have been invited into by the State concerned. If economic diplomacy's function at a national level, is to strengthen the national economy through indigenous means, with the provision of "capacity building" from external sources, then this principle is very important.

Economic diplomacy must be addressed and implemented at three levels: national, regional and international; the Charter does exactly that. Article 7 of the Charter provides, inter alia, that:

> Every State has the primary responsibility to promote the economic, social and cultural development of its people.

Promotion of the economic, social and cultural development of peoples in a State may have to be achieved with external help in the form of "capacity building" for which economic diplomacy is often needed particularly in choosing what may be described as "capacity builders".

Article 7 of the Charter also provides that:

> … each State has the right and the responsibility to choose its means and goals of development, fully to mobilise and use its resources, to implement progressive economic and social reforms and to ensure the full participation of its people in the process and benefits of development.

The Charter clearly suggests that democratisation of the political system, in particular, would be essential for ensuring the full participation of its peoples in the process of development. The right and responsibility of each State to choose its means and goals of development have been qualified by the statement that implementation of progressive economic and social reforms must be achieved through the full participation of the country's peoples—the democratisation of the process of development. This is where the problem lies in many jurisdictions. The nature of the internal political and economic systems, in particular, directly impacts external relations with other country. This may be described as an important aspect of external economic diplomacy. One of the aspects of "social reform" would be to allow everybody, men or women and every child, access to education and grant any individual his/her basic freedoms. It is elementary that education and knowledge form part of the wealth of a State. Internal socio-economic development in many ways complements the external economic diplomacy for that country, and this also operates as a nexus between domestic socio-economic policy and external economic diplomacy. The latter may not be a success if the other parties in the equation do not think highly of the country initiating economic diplomacy.

Article 8 of the Charter provides a clear direction to diplomats who will work on behalf of their States as to the need for co-operation in facilitating a more rational and equitable international relations. One of the cardinal issues of economic diplomacy is to achieve a "balanced economy in harmony with the needs and interests of all countries."[11] This is an onerous task, but diplomats should take it very seriously and work to achieve this goal as a united front.

Article 8 should be read with Article 9 which provides that all States have the responsibility to "cooperate in the economic, social, cultural, scientific and technological fields for the promotion of economic and social progress throughout the world..." This is another core area for international economic diplomacy. As stated earlier that it is difficult to demonstrate the remit of economic diplomacy, but the promotion of economic and social progress throughout the world is an integral aspect of it, and in fact, one of its goals too.

There exist however two problems in achieving these goals: (a) the lack of co-operation based on historical differences, or differences emanating from religion, political attitudes or for any other reasons; and (b) there

[11] Article 8 of the Charter.

does not exist any binding international convention requiring a knowledgeable country to pass her knowledge to other countries, in particular, developing countries. Much work at a diplomatic level is needed on these issues. The road from enmity to friendship is difficult to traverse, but it can be achieved; and if not achieved, then diplomacy fails everybody. Whether it is an international convention or simply a UN General Assembly resolution or a Declaration, Member Countries of the UN should initiate such an instrument whereby transmission of knowledge from the more knowledgeable to the less knowledgeable becomes a common practice.

Irrespective of the nature of diplomacy, whether general or economic, Members of the UN have the right "to participate fully and effectively in the international decision-making process in the solution of world economic, financial and monetary problems ... through the appropriate international organisations."[12] Often the lack of "bargaining power" on the part of developing countries, in general, is put forward as an excuse for non-participation of developing States in international decision-making process. But, unfortunately, the concept of "bargaining power" is often misconceived; it stands for the power to negotiate.[13]

If international organisations are power-based then that should be corrected first through effective negotiation processes, and there are examples to justify this observation. Despite initial opposition from developed countries, the UN General Assembly Resolution entitled Permanent Sovereignty over Natural Resources, 1962[14] which was initiated by a developing country and supported by many subsequently eventually formed part of customary rules of international law. By the same token, the concept of the Exclusive Economic Zone which has been incorporated into the UN Convention on the Law of the Sea, 1982 was also devised by a developing country. Developing countries have also taken a very effective initiative in regard to the protection of the environment, for example, Stockholm Declaration of 1972 and the Rio Declaration of 1992.

If the world is to be governed and controlled by "muscle power" then there hardly exists any reason for engaging in diplomacy; there would be

[12] Article 10 of the Charter.

[13] See further C Chatterjee, *International Law and Diplomacy* op. cit., at 90.

[14] UNGA Resolution 1803 (XXII) of 1962.

no room for negotiation either. Put simply, if this be the reality, then there would be no need for international and intergovernmental organisations either. One then returns to the "ruler and the ruled" situation which was not envisaged when the UN was set up in 1945.

Article 10 of the Charter of Economic Rights and Duties of State therefore rightly pointed out the need for "participatory" decision-making process within international organisations whereby the interests and rights of all the Member States would be protected rather than being governed by one group of States. The current perception of diplomacy thus needs reviewing.

It is reiterated that economic diplomacy at an international level is mainly concerned with framework policies, guidelines, etc. based on consensus attained through negotiations embracing most of the issues and concerns pertaining to a matter, and in such circumstances, the popular perception[15] of "bargaining power" has very little to do. It would be tragic to mix power politics with economic diplomacy, as in so doing, countries will encourage cartelisation of products or commodities and price fixing etc. "Bargaining power" is to be learned or gained through rationalisation of issues in a balanced way; it does not automatically come to anybody.

It is through the bargaining power of States, both rich and poor, that the changing needs of international economic co-operation may be met. In view of the fast-changing international economic scenarios, diplomats should develop more framework resolutions at the UN level so that States become able to cope with the changing demands of international economic diplomacy.

Article 12 should be read with Article 14 of the Charter. Whereas Article 12 promotes the establishment of sub-regional, regional and inter-regional cooperation arrangements in the pursuit of their economic and social development, Article 14 provides for trade liberalisation. If one looks at EU's trade relationship with third countries (non-EU States) one should be able to establish that save the stronger third States, namely, Australia, Canada, New Zealand or the United States, EU allows limited market access to other third countries. Article 14 provides for progressive dismantling of obstacles to trade and "... the improvement of the international framework for the conduct of world trade." This is where

[15] Emphasis added.

diplomatic negotiations at an international platform, such as the World Trade Organization (WTO) and/or UN Conference on Trade and Development (UNCTAD) becomes essential. This Article further provides that:

> … States shall take measures aimed at securing additional benefits for the international trade of developing countries so as to achieve a substantial increase in their foreign exchange earnings, the diversification of their exports, the acceleration of the rate of growth of their trade, taking into account their development needs, an improvement in the possibilities for these countries to participate in the expansion of world trade …

The provisions of Article 14 are directly concerned with economic diplomacy. Trade, both domestic and foreign have traditionally been a primary source of income for countries. It is therefore important that this source of income does not become subject to obstacles, internal and/or external. Whereas internal controls may be imposed by a Sovereign State for reasons of particular national interest, for example, trade in timber (with a view not to encouraging deforestation), the international community should take proactive action for the liberalisation of export trade by ensuring that hindrances to such trade are not raised. These hindrances may be raised by regional trading blocs or by special arrangements between States. Whereas the European Union is an example of the former, the North American Free Trade Area (NAFTA) serves as an example of the latter. The tripartite NAFTA Agreement (the US, Canada and Mexico) has expanded the markets for each of its Member States, and the two richer Member States, Canada and the United States, in effect, derive most benefits.

In order to improve the international framework for the conduct of world trade, diplomats belonging to both developed and developing countries should develop new policies and framework for import–export trade and investments bearing in mind that the emerging markets are now the new players in markets, and that their trade and investment policies should be taken into consideration in developing trade and investment policies for other countries too. The New International Economic Order (NIEO) formulated in 1974, needs reviewing in order to accommodate the aspirations and capabilities of these players. The dynamics of import–export trade and private foreign investment has changed.

China and India are currently investing in those countries in which many traditional investors have not invested in the past; alternatively, they are investing on new terms, based on co-operation agreements, which was not very evident in the world of investments dominated by investors (usually transnational corporations) of developed countries. The issue of dominating the markets and the world of investment by transnational corporations or even by other forms of investors would not arise; thus, these investors are required to accept the terms and conditions of the traditional markets in the West. The question remains whether transnational corporations, as private foreign investors, should not be subject to similar restrictions in developing countries, for example, through screening laws and appropriate investment and related legislations. Unless developing countries, in general, have minimised the judicial risk, and developed reliable administrative systems, it would be difficult for them to attract or raise the volume of private foreign investments. Thus, these background checks have to be completed first by developing countries before inviting transnational corporations into their countries. What may be described as a "balancing of interest" has to be struck first. Here, economic diplomacy should be at its best. What developed countries should also realise is that unless developing countries are developed by them speedily so that the latter's purchasing capacity increases, developed countries will have very limited markets.

However, Article 14 has created a dilemma in regard to trade liberalisation, whereas it provides, inter alia, that:

> ... all States should co-operate, inter alia, towards the progressive dismantling of obstacles to trade and the improvement of the international framework for the conduct of world trade...

Article 12(1) states inter alia, that:

> States have the right, in agreement with the parties concerned, to participate in sub-regional, regional and interregional co-operation in the pursuit of their economic and social development.

But, of course, this Article also provided a caveat by stating that:

> All States engaged in such co-operation have the duty to ensure that the policies of those groupings to which they belong correspond to the provisions of the present Charter and are outward looking, consistent with their international obligations and with the needs of international economic co-operation...

Examples of some of the other regional economic arrangements would be the ANDEAN Pact, the ASEAN, and the MERCOSUR. Basically, these economic co-operation arrangements tend to do trade among their Member States on a preferential trading arrangement.

It is to be emphasised that despite creating a dilemma between the idea of promoting world trade and regional and sub-regional trading arrangements, the Charter through Article 12, on balance, tilted the balance towards outward looking trade which would be consistent with their international obligations. Inclusive regional trading arrangements may raise trade barriers rather than dismantling them, and that will be contrary to the spirit of the Charter of Economic Rights and Duties of States.

The principal theme of Article 13 is about the benefits that are to be derived from transfers of foreign technology. The primary objectives of acquiring foreign technology are: (a) to accelerate socio-economic development of developing host countries by building their capacity to develop indigenous technologies of high standards in consequence of which they would eventually be active players on the relevant markets with competitive edge; and (b) to strengthen and develop their scientific and technological infrastructures and scientific research and technological activities in order to enable them to expand and transform their economies. The Charter thus recommends all States to facilitate the access of developing countries to the achievements of modern science and technology.

However, one of the principal and traditional problems in regard to acquisition—transfer of technology has been the issue of the lack of bargaining power of developing countries; they often become subservient to transferors which weakens their position even more. This is a matter of applying very effective negotiating techniques of recipients of technology. Technology market is imperfect in that it is not governed by any predetermined pricing system; prices are fixed by and through sheer bargaining power.[16] This report also identifies the strategies of technology acquisition by acquirers of technology. These have been clearly identified in that Report.

The current practice of the transfer of technology from the developed to the developing countries has provoked much controversy. In an attempt to correct this practice, the UN Conference on Trade and Development (UNCTAD) published a Draft Code of Conduct on Transfer of Technology which is worth considering. There exists yet another problem on this issue—until date, the international community has not contended any binding international convention which would oblige developed countries to transfer knowledge to developing countries, although it is done by countries on a bi-lateral basis only in a limited number of cases. Out of the reasons which hinders transfer of the appropriate technology to developing countries is, in general, their lack of absorption capacity. It is a cyclical problem in that unless technology is acquired, the indigenous people may not be able to increase their absorption capacity; on the other hand, they are unable to acquire technology often owing to the lack of funds required for the acquisition of the most appropriate technology for their purpose. This issue urgently needs the attention of governments and diplomats in developing countries.

Article 15 of the Charter refers to a fundamentally important issue which is the link between disarmament and the lack of socio-economic development in a country. Socio-economic development in a country depends upon a variety of factors which may be internal or external in nature. Both the use and abuse of armaments directly contributes to hindering the progress or process of socio-economic development in any country, let alone developing countries. Article 15 therefore recommends States, inter alia, to achieve a complete disarmament under effective international control, and to utilise the resources used on armaments to socio-economic development of countries.

This issue should be treated as an issue of "international concern", and diplomats are required to lobby it at all levels, national, regional and international. By the same token, the drafters of the Charter decided to include apartheid, racial discrimination, colonialism and neo-colonialism and all forms of foreign aggression, occupation, domination, etc., so that these could be eliminated urgently as otherwise they would pose hindrances to

[16] See further the Report of the Committee on Transnational Corporations, op. cit.

socio-economic development process. This Article is particularly based on the example of South Africa in which apartheid was rampant at the material time. There were objections from certain quarters as to the relevance of this Article to the Charter. These objections may be answered in the following ways: (a) that apartheid was interwoven in the South African economy, and should not witness that kind of situation anywhere else. It was a direct protest against the contemporary regime of South Africa and (b) that it has been the policy of the United Nations to include an unacceptable issue in documents where possible and relevant to register its abhorrence against such a practice.

This Charter attempted to achieve two main objectives: (a) to identify the issues of international economic law and diplomacy that need the attention of the international community; and (b) to request the international community to pay particular attention to developing countries in their efforts to accelerate their economic development process.

Article 17 provides, inter alia, that international co-operation for development is "... the shared goal and common duty of all States". Thus, it expects every State's co-operation to maintain the aspirations of developing countries whereby their economic and social development process would be accelerated by providing, among others, favourable external conditions, which would principally mean pulling down barriers to trade.

In reinforcing the ideas enshrined in Article 17 of this Charter, Article 18 provided that developed countries should:

> ... extend, improve and enlarge the system of generalised non-recipient and non-discriminatory tariff preferences to the developing countries...

This Charter also recommends that developed States should seriously consider whether they should not allow developing countries other differential measures and the most favoured nation treatment when they may engage in transnational trade. Developed countries in conducting international economic relations should endeavour to avoid measures "... having a negative effect on the development of the national economies of the developing countries..."[17]

Although Article 18 encourages developed States to extend, improve and enlarge the system of generalised non-reciprocal and non-discriminatory tariff preferences (GSP) to developing countries, it should

[17] Article 18 of the Charter.

however be pointed out that GSP is not a panacea to the hindrances that developing countries, in general, encounter in transnational trade. Under the general GSP system a developing country when engaged in transnational trade with a developed country granting of GSP will not be required to pay any tariff to gain access to the markets of that developed country; however, when the developed country would like to gain access to the markets of that developing country, it will be required to pay tariff on the products in conformity with schedule of tariffs developed by the developing country concerned. GSP schemes are operated by the UN and the EU, for example. The categories of products on which GSPs are granted are determined by the grantor States; furthermore, these preferences are allowed on an annual basis in consequence of which the countries having the privilege of GSP may not expect a renewal of these preferences; from this point of view, the system may produce a "de-stabilising" effect on the country which was once allowed GSP. The categories of products on which GSP may have been allowed may also change every year.

The GSP grantor States have the discretion to disallow a former GSP-privileged country this privilege at any time, usually of course on the grounds of the national interest or owing to deterioration of the political relations between the grantor and the licensee.[18] Article 18 should be read with Article 19. On the other hand, it should be borne in mind that it is not only by aid, trade preferences in whatever form these might be, that socio-economic development may be achieved. What is essential is to negotiate for "capacity building" which would lessen dependency on rich economies and allow developing countries to achieve economic self-sufficiency. Indeed, in Article 22(3) the Charter provides that:

> The flow of development assistance resources should include economic and technical assistance.

Socio-economic development should be achieved through indigenous means, wherever possible. Developing countries may find it useful to achieve "modernisation".

In Articles 20, 21 and 23 the Charter recommends developing countries to do the following: (a) in their efforts to increase their overall trade,

[18] See further S K Chatterjee, "Forty Years of International Action for Trade Liberalization", op. cit.

they should pay due attention "... to the possibility of expanding their trade with socialist countries, by granting to these countries conditions for trade not inferior to those granted normally to the developed market economy countries"[19] and (b) these countries should also endeavour to promote the expansion of their mutual trade, grant trade preferences to other developing countries, without being obliged to extend such preferences to developed countries provided "these arrangements do not constitute an impediment to general trade liberalisation and expansion" (Article 21). These countries should enhance the effective mobilisation of their own resources and in order to achieve this, they should strengthen their economic co-operation and expand their mutual trade (Article 23).

The Charter requested the international community, especially its developed Member States, to pay special attention to the particular needs and problems of the least developed States, the land-locked and island developing countries in order to enable them to overcome their particular difficulties which would, in turn, contribute to their socio-economic development.[20]

Through its Article 26, the Charter makes an emotional appeal to the international community, the rationale behind which is sustainable, but unfortunately, given the current attitudes of the major players, on the world stage, this appeal may not be materialised in the near future. It provides, inter alia, that:

> All States have the duty to co-exist in tolerance and live together in peace, irrespective of differences in political, economic, social and cultural systems, and to facilitate trade between States having different economic and social systems.

The Charter's aspirations can be materialised provided the world community believes that it is not by warfares that peace can be brought into this world, and that without democratic governance socio-economic development cannot take place, and that without socio-economic development peace cannot be established.

The remaining Articles in Chapter II of the Charter, Articles 27 and 28 are primarily concerned with the expansion of world trade and world economy, the progressive role of developing countries in world invisible

[19] Article 20 of the Charter.

[20] Article 25 of the Charter.

trade, adjustments in the prices of exports of developing countries in relation to prices of imports and to work out a formula by the international community which would be "remunerative for producers and equitable for producers and consumers".[21]

Chapter III of the Charter (Articles 29 and 30) deals with a novel theme, namely, Common Responsibilities Towards the International Community. Article 29 provides, inter alia, that:

> The sea-bed and ocean floor and the subsoil thereof, beyond the limits of national jurisdiction, as well as the resources of the area, are the common heritage of mankind.
>
> ... all States shall ensure that the exploration of the area and exploitation of its resources are carried out exclusively for peaceful purposes and that the benefits derived therefrom are shared equitably by all States ...

In recent years, the concept of the Common Heritage of mankind was consolidated by the Moon Treaty of 1969. In order to protect the interest of the land-locked States as to resources available and exploited in the High Seas, the UN Convention on the Law of the Sea (UNCLOS III) the Seabed Authority has been authorised to protect the interests of these States in respect of those resources. In other words, in this respect, the aspirations of the Charter have been materialised.

Article 30 of the Charter refers to a very important issue on which the international community's urgent attention is needed—the environmental problems. It is worth quoting the text of the entire Article:

> The protection, preservation and enhancement of the environment for the present and future generations is the responsibility of all States. All States shall endeavour to establish their own environmental and developmental policies in conformity with such responsibility. The environmental policies of all States should enhance and not adversely affect the present and future development potential of developing countries. All States have the responsibility to ensure that activities within their jurisdiction or control do not cause damage to the environment of other States or of areas beyond the limits of national jurisdiction. All States should co-operate in evolving international norms and regulations in the field of the environment.

[21] Article 28 of the Charter.

What the drafters envisaged in Article 30 as early as 1974, is still true; unfortunately, the progress of the international community on this issue still remains at an unsatisfactory level, one of the reasons for this may be attributed to the lack of "public awareness" in addition to the lack of regulatory measures owing to the shortage of qualified enforcement officers in many jurisdictions. It is an issue to which diplomats should also pay their urgent attention to mobilise public opinion at national levels and attempt to implement international norms at domestic levels.

Article 31 of the Charter states that all States "… have the duty to contribute to the balanced expansion of the world economy … and the fact that the prosperity of the international community as a whole depends upon the prosperity of its constituent parts"—meaning thereby of the both developed and developing countries.

What was stated in Article 32 is still valid, and needs no explanation:

> No State may use or encourage the use of economic, political or any other type of measures to coerce another State in order to obtain from it the subordination of the exercise of its sovereign rights.

4.4 Conclusions

The Charter of Economic Rights and Duties of States, 1974 identified most of the important issues relating to economic rights and duties of States. It is quite a comprehensive instrument in relation to the themes of it.

One of the themes that cuts across the Charter is the interrelationship between trade and development. The Charter remains as an "isolated" instrument even though most of its provisions, except those which are concerned with the issue of payment of compensation in the event of taking of foreign assets (Article 2(c)), cartelisation of commodity markets and control over their price-fixing (Articles 5 and 6) and the issue of apartheid (Article 16). It is maintained that barring these provisions, the provisions of the Charter are acceptable, and the international community could have accepted and implemented the rest of the Charter.

There also exists the view that such a resolution can only create what is known as "soft law"; thus, these provisions have really no binding effect and that this kind of resolutions, even if accepted by the international community can only give rise to "soft law". One should appreciate that soft law often can be harder than the hard law. Take, for example, the

Codes of Conduct to regulate the conduct of various professions in the UK. They are not parliamentary legislation; yet breach of these Codes of Conduct gives rise to claims; thus, it would be foolish not to accept them by various professions.

Academic views on this issue are divergent.[22] There are examples to establish that some other resolutions of the UN, namely, the Permanent Sovereignty over Natural Resources of 1962 or the Uniting for Peace Resolution of 1950 or the Declaration on the Granting of Independence to Colonial Countries and Peoples, 1960 are binding. By not accepting the acceptable provisions of the Charter of Economic Rights and Duties of States, 1974, the international community has taken one step backwards rather than forward.[23]

This Charter which primarily identifies the basic issues with which international economic diplomacy is concerned also provides guidance to its users as to what should be achieved by them as diplomats. The issue of whether this instrument is legally binding or not is unnecessary because it should be treated as a "directive" to diplomats and any others who may be willing to learn what international economic diplomacy is all about. Of course, it is for the members of the international community to develop their international economic policies based on the ideas provided for by the Charter. It is interesting to note that although drafted over forty years ago, its contents are in most cases still valid.

[22] See further D H N Johnson, "The Effect of Resolutions of the General Assembly of the United Nations", 32 *British Year Book of International Law* (1955–56) 97; but see also B Sloane, "The Binding Force of a Recommendation of the General Assembly of the United Nations" 25 *British Year Book of International Law* (1948) 14.

[23] See further S K Chatterjee, "The Charter of Economic Rights and Duties of States: An Evaluation after 15 Years", 40 *International and Comparative Law Quarterly*, 669 at 681.

CHAPTER 5

Economic Diplomacy and Commercial Diplomacy

5.1 Introduction

Whereas in the world of diplomacy, commercial diplomacy is a known concept, the concept of economic diplomacy may not be so common. Commercial diplomacy has been with the world of diplomacy probably since the days of bi-lateral inter-nation commercial relationship for the purpose of expanding trade and business between themselves. Economic diplomacy, as has been explained in this chapter, is much broader than commercial diplomacy; its primary objective is to develop policies for economic relations between sovereign States and to make the bases for inter-State economic relations fair and equitable.

Both commercial diplomacy and economic diplomacy require very good skills in negotiating techniques, and it has been explained in this chapter what type of diplomats would be best suited for each of these types of diplomacy. This chapter also attempts to explain how developing countries may be able to strengthen their position at various international fora.

5.2 Examining the Differences Between Economic Diplomacy and Commercial Diplomacy

Economic diplomacy is primarily concerned with policy-making for economic security of a country by diplomacy and through diplomatic negotiations. These negotiations can take place at bi-lateral and

C. Chatterjee, *Economic Diplomacy and Foreign Policy-making*,
https://doi.org/10.1007/978-3-030-49047-8_5

multilateral bases. Whereas bi-lateral negotiations which take place between two States, for example, for securing private foreign investment opportunities, or technology transfer or for any other venture between the two States concerned, economic diplomacy at a multilateral platform, such as regional bodies or the UN agencies, aims at developing new rules of State conduct or what should be achieved by the members of the international community for international development in the proper sense of the term. It requires a genuine international co-operation of the international community, examples of which are rather abysmally few.

Commercial diplomacy, on the other hand, is concerned with commercial matters, including transnational deals, e.g. import–export trade or trade preferences negotiated between two States or any other deals or privileges of a commercial/transactional nature. Commercial diplomacy is primarily developed on a bi-lateral or on a regional arrangement of an economic, or a socio-economic nature.

Commercial diplomacy has a much narrower base than economic diplomacy; the latter is more concerned with policy-making on a wider basis, such as the discussion at a diplomatic level, for example, the Uruguay Round which eventually led to the establishment of the World Trade Organization (WTO). Whereas economic diplomacy is, in the main, concerned with mutual benefit-making, commercial diplomacy is primarily aimed at profit-making on a bi-lateral or multilateral basis. Commercial diplomacy may also be defined as an activity conducted by diplomats with a view to promoting business between a home and a host State.

This definition does affirm that the main objective of commercial diplomacy is to encourage business development rather than policy-making. In commercial diplomacy usually commercial counsellors, commercial attachés or commercial/trade representatives are engaged. Commercial diplomacy should be directed, where possible, at devising projects which would require both (partners from developed and developing) parties to work together for mutual benefit, e.g. under the buy-back system.

Economic diplomacy entails using traditional diplomatic tools such as lobbying, representation, negotiation and promotion of further economic policies of the State. Economic diplomacy may also be described as an economic craft. In economic diplomacy, diplomats must have special knowledge of the economic needs of their country, and in the negotiation process, capacity building of the country must be emphasised as a major issue. The Charter of Economic Rights and Duties of States,

1974, which was further supplemented by the Doha Declaration of 2001 are two exemplary documents to learn the issues with which economic diplomacy is concerned. The primary aspects of these two important documents have already been discussed in Chapter 4 of this work. It is for diplomats to develop more binding guidelines along the lines of the UN General Assembly Resolution entitled Permanent Sovereignty over Natural Resources, 1962.

Commercial diplomacy seems to have received a kind of secondary status in the world of diplomacy, in that "diplomacy" has traditionally been regarded as a vehicle for developing foreign relations between States without realising that it is economic diplomacy of which commercial diplomacy is part; thus, as stated before, commercial diplomats, who, in State practice, has been described differently by different States, namely, "commercial representative", "economic counsellor", "commercial counsellor", "trade representative" etc.;[1] furthermore, certain matters of commercial diplomacy are assigned to external organisations by Missions; this practice implies two things: (a) that either the Mission concerned is too busy to be engaged in commercial activities; or (b) that their staff may lack negotiating skills in dealing with commercial matters. From either point of view, this situation, if it exists within a Mission should be avoided, for it has already been stated that commercial diplomacy, which is part of economic diplomacy, in a significant way impacts the foreign policy-making of a country.

The balance between economic diplomacy including commercial diplomacy and foreign policy-making needs to be struck. Commercial importance of a country in a receiving State often determines the size of the foreign Mission in the latter. Examples of this are available in all receiving States. Though interactions between commercial and economic matters both in the sending State and receiving State may be able to come closer to each other, and indeed, inter-dependent on each other. The lesser State should, through effective negotiation, with the stronger State (the receiving State) can achieve what may be described as "capacity building". The reality is that if developing countries fail to do so, then they themselves will create diplomacy of dependency.[2]

[1] M Kostecki and O Naray, *Commercial Diplomacy and International Business*, The Netherlands Institute for International Relations (2007).

[2] See further C Chatterjee, *International Law and Diplomacy*, London, Routledge (2011) at 117–129.

5.3 Challenges for Developing Sending and Receiving States

There exist certain deep-rooted problems and issues in traditional diplomacy, which is not entirely relevant to the contemporary world. Traditional diplomacy has, in many ways, failed to cope with the demands of the contemporary world of diplomacy primarily because it has not been moving forward as fast as it was expected. The old diplomatic protocol is still relevant, but review of it in respect of certain issues has proved to be very important. The selection process, the knowledge in political science, economics, security issues and more importantly the role of the UN, including its agencies and the training needed for representing the country's interest before it, the rule-making procedure by it, and how regional needs should be presented to name but a few. To lay these deficiencies in the current diplomatic world is a daunting task, but the developing and the middle-grade States should reflect on this issue.

Developing sending and receiving States have significant potentials—these potentials, both in the forms of natural and human resources must be effectively utilised. Unfortunately, human resources in these countries are not utilised to their optimum level. It would be beyond the scope of this work to discuss those issues; but one issue should nevertheless be pointed out that unless peoples within a State are allowed to be participatory, it's politico-economic status will remain low. One cannot any longer live in the colonial past, its adverse impact on colonies may not be forgotten—but one has to turn a new leaf in one's life. It is a difficult road to stride, but it has to be done.

The above statement is made on the behaviour of the developing countries, in general; they have become aid and loan-dependent on other countries, in consequence of which they have lost their voice on international fora, and even at a bi-lateral level. The days of inward-looking and outward-looking strategies, which were propounded by many economists, are over. Unless, nature has become cruel to a developing country, there is no reason why the practice of high importation may not be changed. One can only refer to China and India, and, in particular, the latter. A few years ago, India was highly dependent on importation of food products; now the same country, through well-thought-out policy-making, has become a major exporter of food products. Most of the developing countries still export the age-old products, like tea, coffee, rubber and, of course, natural resources. The course of business and production policies may be changed. Both China and India are now regarded as emerging markets. Commercial divisions of sending developing countries to developed receiving States should change their current policies of what may be described as a two-way benefit policy.[3] This is why the importance of learning effective negotiating techniques has been emphasised in a separate chapter of this work.

Furthermore, the prejudice against countertrade must be overcome. Many countries still regard it as a primitive type of trade, and they want to earn hard currencies (preferably the US dollars) to raise their foreign resources without realising that any high incidence of import trade will adversely affect these reserves. The United Kingdom, one of the richest countries in the world, is heavily engaged in countertrade in various countries, like many others in the world, namely, Australia and many of the countries in the Middle East.[4]

Three other important disciplines, among others, often neglected by regimes in most of the developing countries: banking, an extensive form of business which should contribute to socio-economic development process, including the small and medium industries (SMEs), education, and development of indigenous technology, unfortunately, the latter is a product of prejudice again. Developing countries, in general, may perhaps find it more profitable to develop their own technology rather than depending on used imported technology, which is neither cost-effective nor environmentally friendly. This issue has been developed in a separate chapter of this work.[5]

But, most of all, public awareness, technical skills of human resources (both male and female) must be raised in all these countries. It is elementary to point out that without the development of human resources in all important aspects of life, namely, science, medicine and arts a country may not prosper at all, and by not achieving this kind of development, diplomacy of dependency will precipitate.

[3] See further C Chatterjee, *Legal Aspects of Trade Finance*, London, Routledge (2001) at 11 et seq.

[4] See further *Legal Aspects of Trade Finance*, op. cit., at 9 et seq.

[5] See Chapter 12.

5.4 Conclusions

Whereas Article 3 of the Vienna Convention on Diplomatic Relations, 1961 failed to expand on the functions of diplomatic missions, presumably, in the belief that diplomats and their Missions should be aware of them (which is not necessarily the case), Article 5 of the Vienna Convention on Consular Relations, 1963, on the other hand, refers to the consular functions in good details.

Then comes the issue of trade terms—diplomats including the heads of their commercial departments should pay their urgent and meaningful attention to considering whether the current trend, including the most-favoured nation treatment is still tenable or not.[6] This is a matter which is beyond the remit of this work, but developing countries should reflect on this issue too. Neither the Charter of Economic Rights and Duties of States 1974 nor the Doha Declaration of 2001 has been really implemented by the international community; by implementing some of its key provisions, they could have easily set an example that a Declaration or guidelines (the 1974 Charter) which were predominantly their work, should, in reality, also be effected.

Finally, it is really unfortunate that perhaps except the Association of South East Asian States (ASEAN), none of the other regional economic arrangements set up by developing States has proved to be successful. Regional economic arrangements could have found the platforms for the economic and defence strategies.

[6] See further S K Chatterjee, "Forty Years of International Action for Trade Liberalisation", op. cit.

CHAPTER 6

Emerging Markets and Diplomacy

6.1 Introduction

The emerging economies particularly in Asia and Latin America, namely, Brazil, China and India, are now prepared to compete with the traditional players on the world trade and investment markets. The advent of these economies would require the traditional players to review their transnational business strategies which would enable them to protect their interests, both economic and politico-economic, on the profitable markets. Furthermore, the traditional players are now required to critically examine the trade and investment strategies of the emerging economies.

There should not be any prejudice against the emerging economies that they would not be able to compete against the traditional players. The choice of sectors of economies for investment and the products for trade is worth considering: (a) China like India are investing in the manufacturing service as well as natural resources sectors and (b) they have already established their competitive edge.

Economic diplomacy in regard to emerging economies should be viewed by diplomats from a new perspective. In fact, it is an uncharted field for them. In regard to emerging economies, economic diplomacy presents new challenges for diplomats belonging to both traditional economies and emerging economies.

C. Chatterjee, *Economic Diplomacy and Foreign Policy-making*,
https://doi.org/10.1007/978-3-030-49047-8_6

6.2 The General Characteristics of Emerging Economies and Economic Diplomacy

At the outset, it should be pointed out that each of the emerging economies has its own characteristics which contributed to their socio-economic development process. However, the common characteristics of these economies are the following: they all are primarily agricultural economies with emerging industrial infrastructure; still many industries are labour-intensive, the level of skills is not as high, in general, as in the western economies; their financial infrastructures need to be well-regulated, and that each of these economies has good small-scale industry sector including the sector for handicrafts; furthermore, higher education is elitist in each of these countries.

Currently, each of these three economies is characterised by a high population growth and its attendant impact on the socio-economic dimensions to their societies, but each of them is endowed with both human and natural resources.

6.3 Certain Emerging Market Profiles

6.3.1 Brazil[1]

Brazil is the world's seventh wealthiest economy. Her gross domestic product (GDP) was US$ 2.223 trillion in 2012. Brazil is the largest country in Latin America and the Caribbean with the largest population in that geographic area. Brazil's GDP rose up to 7.5% during 2011 and 2012 but owing to domestic and external factors its economic progress slowed down in the following year. However, the overall economic performance has recently been better with low inflation rates and improvements in social well-being. Brazil's banking system has remained sound, and the flow of foreign direct investment into Brazil seems to have remained more than sufficient to cover any deficits. Brazil has very high level of foreign currency reserves (about US$ 358 billion at the end of 2015). In order to increase investment in infrastructure and provide tax incentives for faster and more robust economic growth, a Growth Acceleration Plan was

[1]The information is derived exclusively from the *World Development Indicators* published by the World Bank Group 2013 and a further Report from the World Bank which covered up to the year 2015. Some of the important statements have also been reproduced from the Indicators in order not to distort them.

launched in 2007, and again in 2012 the government launched a range of initiatives with a view, inter alia, to reducing energy costs, strengthening investment in infrastructure through foreign participation, and restructuring oil royalty payments. All these efforts clearly suggest that Brazil is mindful of keeping the basic factors of economic growth strong and strengthen them periodically.

Despite her efforts to ensure economic growth, the counterbalancing factors in Brazil are the extreme regional differences in the country—particularly between the South and the South East (the richer parts) and the North and the North-East (the poorer parts). However, according to the World Bank Review, poverty fell significantly from 21% of the population in 2003 to 11% in 2009, and extreme poverty also dropped dramatically from 10% in 2004 to 2.25% in 2009, while income growth rate of the poorest 40% rose on average 7.1% between 2003 and 2014. Universal coverage of primary education has been achieved, but the country is still struggling to improve the quality and outcome of the system, especially at the basic and secondary levels. Brazil is still a middle-income country.

The country receives support from the World Bank Group—its 2012–2015 Partnership Strategy guaranteed US$ 5.8 billion in investments for the first two years with a strong focus on the states and large municipalities and redoubled support for the North-East, the country's poorest region. The key features of the Partnership Strategy are to:

- strengthen public and private investment;
- strengthen regional and territorial development;
- improve service delivery to the poor and
- support an effective management of natural resources and the environment.

In September 2013, the IBRD financed 82 active projects, and more finance was made available by the World Bank Group to 23 global environmental projects, carbon finance etc. The World Bank Group focuses on reaching the poorest and achieving higher levels of quality and efficiency in social services, in addition to launching perhaps the best and the most ambitious social protection programme in the world (Bolsa Familia).

The World Bank has been very active in helping states and municipalities in organising result-oriented management practices based on sound fiscal management, for example, Rio de Janeiro Metropolitan Urban and Housing Development project, Minas Gerais Partnership for Development Programme and Rio de Janeiro State Public Sector Modernization Programme. The Bank also acknowledged that in few countries the ecosystem is as crucial to development and people's welfare as in Brazil and also that a significant part of Brazil's economy relies on the use of natural resources. The country is also vulnerable to natural disasters.

The World Bank Group has also been involved in providing assistance to small-scale agriculture and production in innovative ways, which would empower local communities particularly in the poorer areas of the country. Brazil's economic standing has recently deteriorated, but in view of her economic potentials, it has been decided to exemplify the country's profile. However, Brazil's economic and social progress between 2003 and 2014 saved 29 million people out of poverty.

6.3.2 *China*[2]

With the initiation of market reforms in 1978, China shifted from a centrally planned to a market-based economy, as much as possible, as a direct result of which the country at least partially experienced rapid economic and social development; the GDP growth averaged about 10% a year. China is currently the second-largest economy and has adopted outward-looking development and investment strategy. China's presence in the western world has been clearly evident, and she has already established her presence as an investor in certain parts of Asia and Africa.

However, according to the World Bank, China remains a developing country; in 2012 China's GDP per capita was US$ 6264, gross national income per capita was US$ 15.12 trillion and ranked 90th in the world. Poverty in certain parts of China still exists, but the major economic overhaul has lifted 800 million out of poverty.

Recently, rapid economic performance has brought many challenges too, including high inequality, rapid urbanisation and challenges to environmental sustainability. China's 12th Five-Year Plan (2011–2015)

[2] The information is derived exclusively from the *World Development Indicators* published by the World Bank Group 2013 and a further Report from the World Bank which covered up to the year 2015. Some of the important statements have also been reproduced from the Indicators in order not to distort them.

addresses several issues which deserve her urgent attention, namely environmental issues, social imbalances, education and healthcare, social protection etc. The government has recently placed emphasis on quality of life rather than on pace of growth.

Based on the joint study entitled China 2030 prepared by the World Bank and the Development Research Centre of the State Council (China), the World Bank Group focuses on the following areas:

- Support for greener growth—for example, by enhancing urban environmental services, promoting sustainable agriculture practices, demonstrating pollution management and related matters;
- Promotion of more inclusive development—for example, by increasing access to quality health services and social protection, enhancing opportunities in rural areas and small towns, strengthening skills development programmes and
- Advancement of mutually beneficial relations with the world—by supporting South-South co-operation and China's role as a global shareholder.

The World Bank Group's most valuable contribution to China has been in the form of providing and applying ideas, innovation and knowledge. But as of 31 August 2013, the Bank's cumulative lending (IBRD and IDA) to China was more than US$ 2.39 billion for 364 projects on the protection and preservation of the environment, urban development, transportation, rural development, human development, energy and water resources management. The Bank also pays attention to eradication of poverty particularly in the areas/provinces in which poverty is rife. China's 12th Five-year Plan (2011–2015) and the 13th Five-year Plan (2016–2020) addresses issues such as, development of services, environmental and social imbalances, education, health etc.

As China develops, the World Bank is being engaged more and more in collaborative research and analysis, for example, the project entitled Building a Modern, Harmonious and Creative Society of 2030, lays out various strategic directions for China's future—completing the transition to a market economy, accelerating the pace of open innovation, the "green project" relating to the preservation and promotion of the environment, expansion of opportunities and services, such as, education, health and access to jobs for all people; and to seek mutually beneficial relations with the world by reforming China's economic structure to the changing international economy.

As recently as 2013, the International Finance Corporation (IFC) invested more than US$ 1 billion in 32 projects, and IFC's strategic priorities in China focus on climate change, energy efficiency, green policy, water efficiency, food safety etc. Over the past three decades China has significantly reduced her level of poverty and substantial progress has been made in human development indicator.

With the launching of her economic reforms programmes in 1980, China started working in partnership with the World Bank Group which became a source of finance and technical assistance for achieving those economic reforms by adopting modern project management methodologies, and new technologies. Some of the projects which seem to have brought in an overall improvement in China's socio-economic sectors are:

- the Poor Rural Communities Development Project;
- the Ningbo Water and Environmental Project;
- the Loess Plateau Watershed Rehabilitation Project;
- the Renewable Energy Development Project;
- the Basic Education in Western Areas Project and
- the Forestry Development in Poor Areas Project.

The Bank encourages other countries to share knowledge with China, where possible. In 2018 (April) the Bank's cumulative lending (IBRD and IDA) to China was more than US$ 60,495 billion for 416 projects for improvement of transportation, urban and rural developments, energy and water resources management.

6.3.3 India[3]

India is the world's fourth largest economy. Since 1947, that is the year in which India attained her independence, she brought about a landmark agricultural revolution (1974) making the country a major food exporter in the world; life expectancy has more than doubled, literacy rates have

[3]The information is derived exclusively from the *World Development Indicators* published by the World Bank Group 2013 and a further Report from the World Bank which covered up to the year 2015. Some of the important statements have also been reproduced from the Indicators in order not to distort them.

quadrupled and a sizeable middle-class has emerged. It has internationally recognised pharmaceutical, steel and information industries. The country is also known for her advanced space technologies. India will soon have the largest and youngest workforce in the world. It has the largest rural–urban migration in the world.[4]

But, poverty remains a critical problem for India to resolve.[5] The health care system should be universal within the country and it should be free for all, and the same argument may also be applied to the system of education in the country. The country's infrastructure needs are considerable. Certain states in the country are more advanced than the others, and the latter may find it useful to utilise the model set by the former. Both primary and secondary education should be all-pervasive and of good standards.

The current Country Partnership Strategy for India had the World Bank Group's support for four years—between 2013 and 2017. The Bank Group plans to support India with an integrated package of financing, advisory services and knowledge tailored to the needs of individual states. Economic activity is expected to stabilise, maintaining annual GDP growth at 7% in the financial year 2018. Growth is projected to increase 7.4% by the financial year 2020.

The issue of poverty in India has been prioritised, and according to the World Bank Group, poverty would be reduced from 29.8% (2010) to 5.5% by 2030. With the partnership of the World Bank Group with India, the latter will have a platform for growth, to derive benefits from India's spatial transformation and also to increase its human potential. Rural–Urban Transformation, that is, the rural to urban shift should be as productive as possible in terms of growth and liability of urban areas, especially secondary cities where a sizeable population increase is taking place; and Inclusion, that is, the first two factors—integration and rural–urban transformation—can benefit a large part of the population only if human development takes place supported by policies that help make growth "inclusive". The Bank Group will also support the central and state governments in strengthening the following, in particular, nutrition, quality education mainly in the secondary and tertiary

[4] According to the World Development Indicators, about 10 million people move to towns and cities each year in search of jobs and opportunities.

[5] According to the World Development Indicators, about 53 million people came out of poverty level between 2005 and 2010.

levels, opening opportunities in higher education, including education for girls at secondary level and social protection.[6]

6.4 Comments

From the above discussion of the three emerging economies, it would be possible to maintain that there may exist any causal connection between a market being "emerging" and its domestic socio-economic conditions. In fact, this was also true of the colonial powers when they started colonising different parts of the world—their own domestic socio-economic conditions were not, in many instances, remarkably good. In fact, the Victorian England has been described by many as a not-so developed country in respect of many domestic issues.[7]

Emerging markets have a huge task to complete—strengthening their domestic socio-economic problems. In fact, as stated earlier, these economies have to perform very well both internally and externally, a "double task" for them. However, as long as their competitiveness exists on the world markets, they should benefit from their new ventures. The emergent economies, as agents of investments, will be required to be more understanding than the traditional investors as the newly born countries' perception of investors' duties have significantly changed; they will be required to invest in a "participatory" manner, and this has been explained in the section entitled "Emerging Markets and Diplomacy".

Based on these characteristics, it would be possible to draw the following inferences:

- that without an all-pervasive education system, economic performance of a country may not be improved; but it is hastened to add that an all-pervasive education system is what is expected of all countries, as it is a factor of socio-economic development. Of course, on the other hand, one can always argue that during the age of the Industrial Revolution in Great Britain, education was not all-pervasive in the British society; but for the continuing and

[6] For the financial contribution and financial assistance provided by the World Bank Group to India on various projects, see World Development Indicators, relating to India (2013) published by the World Bank.

[7] See for example, R Floud, *The People and the British Economy, 1830–1914*, Oxford, Oxford University Press (1997).

progressive development of an economy, an all-pervasive education system would be essential.
- that emerging economies the lack of a full-fledged infrastructure—health, communication, education, transportation etc. which may have a direct impact on their continuing progress.
- that emerging economies do not seem to follow the basic formula of maintaining economic stability, namely, more employment gives rise to more income, and more income leads to more savings and finally, more savings lead to more investments.
- that emerging economies aim at achieving domestic development through investment abroad, a kind of policy, colonial powers pursued during the colonial period. External sources of income will be deployed for domestic socio-economic development, although it is too early to predict the efficacy of these policies in this regard.
- that it is important to bear in mind that in view of the developed world's own industrial capabilities, it would be difficult for the emerging economies to dominate those markets, unless of course, the latter enjoys excellent expertise to reach the expected standards of goods/products, and price differentials. Thus, in respect of certain products and services emerging markets may not be the effective players on the traditional rich markets.
- that in regard to FDI (Foreign Direct Investment) China and India are currently investing rather aggressively in Africa and the Middle East respectively, but these investors have to bear it in mind that investments without any ethics will have a counterproductive effect on the investors. "Ethics" in this context would stand for the contribution that private foreign investors may make to beneficiary countries in the form of training, capacity building for the indigenous people in the form of BOT (Build, Operate and Transport) or BOOT (Build, Own, Operate and Transport). This is a matter of economic diplomacy based on sound negotiating techniques in commercial/investment contracts. This issue has received attention in a different chapter in this work.[8]
- that the geographic area of a population in each of the currently emerging economies are very large, although demands for products, compared to the demand structures in the rich world may not be

[8] Chapter 8.

comparable, but the situation should rapidly change to cause even more anxieties for the West. In his work entitled Storm, Vincent Cable described these countries as "dormant volcanoes coming to life."[9] In order to justify his acronym for these dormant volcanoes, Cable pointed out that it is normal that these two countries each of which accounts for 20% of the world's population should dominate the world economy.[10]

- Relying on Angus Maddison's work,[11] Cable convincingly stated that two centuries ago, China and India respectively accounted for around 35 and 20% of the world population and 30 and 16% of world GDP whereas the US accounts for only 1% of the world population and 2% of the world GDP.[12]
- that both the countries slipped from their respective status for obvious reasons: whereas China decided to live in what may be described as "political isolationism", India became a victim of colonisation. Despite economic and scientific potentials, both the countries were required to go through a long spell of non-outward-looking (or inward-looking) economic strategies. The issue of economic diplomacy did not arise during this period. But prior to the nineteenth century, the dominance of the Asian powers could not be questioned. Brazil, though full of resources went through a similar ordeal. Furthermore, in Brazil, the issue of the lack of socio-cohesiveness has dominated the successive political regimes.
- that whereas India, since she attained her political independence in 1947, has been engaged in implementing democracy in its fullest form (pervasive education being one of the most important factors combined with eradication of poverty) but maintained her progressive development in scientific inventions and innovations coupled with her attempts to test and apply new business models, China, which bear similar characteristics, in general, has been achieving these under a command structure particularly since the 1980s.

[9] V Cable, *The Storm: The World Economic Crisis & What It Means*, London, Atlantic Books (2010) at 94.

[10] V Cable, ibid.

[11] A Maddison, *Monitoring the World Economy 1820–1992*, OECD Development Centre (1995).

[12] V Cable, ibid.

- that in the emerging markets (Brazil, China and India) although human resources are not harnessed to their fullest extent, and that their economic prosperity which would very much depend upon the availability of markets, both domestic and foreign, seems to have been achieved by the participation of the elite minorities.
- that cheap labour and cheap raw materials have directly contributed to their being emerging markets in addition to the outward-looking economic and business strategies that they adopted particularly since the beginning of the twenty-first century.[13]
- that by the time the emerging economies emerged, the majority of the Western markets achieved sophistication in finance, trade and manufacturing of a variety of products; thus the emerging economies managed to attain a comparable capacity at least in certain industries which allowed them to gain slices of markets in the Western world; furthermore, they also attained competence in certain limited sectors, such as IT, mining, exploitation of natural resources and a variety of manufacturing industries.
- that in their becoming emerging markets, the countries concerned generally maintained their respective national business policies, though modified in certain cases, such as management style or more application of technology than maintaining the practice of labour-intensive policies, and an aggressive marketing and investment policy.
- that the emerging economies have gained business grounds predominantly in those of the geographic areas and economic sectors, which developed countries, in general, would not find profitable to enter particularly because of their high labour and incidental costs including those of raw materials and equipment.
- that the emerging economies now present a dilemma in that whereas traditionally they have been aid-receivers, now they are aid-providers to some of the richest countries in the world, a very large lending to the US by China is but one example; accumulation of large foreign reserves by both India and China, whether by virtue of strong export trade based on lower costs of production and yet qualitative products to satisfy the standards of the markets in the West, coupled with their

[13] In this context, see also views of V Cable in *China and India: The New Giants*, London, The Royal Institute of International Affairs (1996); see also Martin Jacques, *When China Rules the World*, London, Allen Lane (2009), and R Kaplinsky, *Globalisation, Poverty and Inequality*, England, Polity Press (2005).

foreign investment-based income enabled them to reach this stage, and this process also largely applies to Brazil.

- that there may not be any causal link between accumulation of foreign exchange reserve by virtue of industrial growth and an all-pervasive socio-economic development in a country, but as stated earlier that these symptoms were also available during the eighteenth and nineteenth centuries in Great Britain and France, as well as in other colonising powers.
- that emerging markets with their often-limited capacities are required to achieve their industrial and innovative sophistications so as to be able to compete with the established economies in the West which phenomenon was not present when the colonial powers started gaining markets in their colonies.
- that by the same token, this competitive industrial strength of the emerging economies albeit in a limited number of economic sectors presents a formidable threat to the traditionally rich countries in the West.
- that it has become manifest in emerging economies so far that without being an "all-rounder", or even a "limited rounder" but with an appropriate level of expertise and innovative ideas may be able to compete with the "all-rounders" at least during the initial stage.
- that emerging markets, in general, have accorded more priorities to outward-looking strategies rather than striking a balance between these two strategies whereby pervasive education and internal infrastructure development, which are symptoms of rich economies may simultaneously take place.
- that in emerging economies human resources usually remain under-utilised in consequence of which they remain less inventive and innovative compared to the traditionally rich countries.
- that emerging economies seem to have realised that a stable government in whatever form is a sine qua non of economic and industrial growth, and that growth must emanate from within rather than growth based on external-dependency.
- that like the traditionally rich countries in the West, emerging economies also believe in "consumerism".
- that emerging economies believe that the State must be allowed to play a dominant role in socio-economic activities within its national boundaries, and beyond.

that the emerging economies, particularly China and India, have deliberately and in a planned manner, kept their currency value depressed in an attempt to increase their export trade, which has directly contributed to increasing their foreign exchange resources.

6.5 The Nature of Competitiveness Between the Traditionally Rich Economies and the Emergent Economies

There is no doubt that these two types of economy are not at par in many respects, and yet they are not competitors. Whereas emerging economies have traditionally remained agricultural in nature with its attendant characteristics, and gradually attained sophistication in certain industries and had to meet with a formidable challenge from the traditional competitors with enviable competence and excellence in industries and investments.

However, the emerging markets, despite their socio-politico and economic problems, which deserve their urgent attention, have decided to become participants in the world market being encouraged by their own achievements. But the advantages that the emerging economies have over the traditionally rich economies is that the former becomes competitive primarily price-wise by virtue of having lower labour costs. The point remains however that with the rise of labour costs, and perhaps the costs of materials, the emerging markets may not be able to maintain their competitiveness unless they excel qualitatively with the corresponding goods or services provided by the traditionally strong economies.

On the other hand, if two forces work hand in hand—cheap labour and scientific invention and innovation—then emerging markets will have a predictable future on the world markets. But, cheap labour may be a temporary phenomenon for two reasons: (a) the urge for comparative wage level, that is, what the rich countries usually offer their labour force and (b) the issue of the awareness of fundamental rights, which might produce a destabilising effect on the existing regimes.

The other important factor to provide competitiveness would be the treatment towards host States by private foreign investors, that is, transnational corporations or even government-controlled foreign investments. Usually, foreign investors have the apprehension that their interests in developing host countries might not receive protection during the life of their investments, which apprehension, in view of their records particularly since 1984 should be reviewed; the traditional host countries would not like to see that private foreign investors do not directly contribute to their benefits in the form of training in industries and capacity building.

Developing countries are now in a position to choose their investors either from the traditionally rich countries or from the emerging economies—who may provide them more benefits than the traditional investors. The aspirations of the emerging economies should not be undermined. On the other hand, the question remains whether emerging markets may march forward without improving and modernising the other sectors of their economy, namely, banking, insurance, high technological training and pervasive education. Emerging markets have thus a two-fold task on their hands: (a) to stay as emerging markets with their current policies of penetrating foreign markets and (b) to strengthen their economic foundation by working on the areas stated above.

6.6 Should Emerging Economies Be Westernised or Modernised?

The differences between "westernisation" and "modernisation" are significant; whereas the former stands for "imitating the west" and adopt their practice and ideology, the latter denotes the idea of being modern over the traditional, although the process might entail a degree of borrowing ideas from the West. Whereas "modernisation" entails a process of upgrading things—industries, education system or health system, for example, through indigenous efforts, "westernisation" is a process which might supplant the indigenous model or structure altogether or superimpose a "foreign" model or structure which might not suit or fit the indigenous structure.

During the colonial period, most of the colonial powers made their best efforts to convert the colonies according to their ideologies but in most cases with limited success. They succeeded in most cases in converting the education system and structure and regulation of commerce, but education did not become "universal" within the colonies; they were required to learn western language, economics, history and geography.

At the cost of their own cultural heritage and excellence, colonial peoples, in general, fell to become disciples of their colonial masters. Conversion of non-Christians to Christianity still remains as a glaring example. The material facilities provided for by the colonial powers to their colonised peoples must have some effect on the minds of the ordinary people to aspire for westernisation, which influence would obviously be rejected by the pioneers of decolonisation. On the other hand, as explained before, the Western or colonial powers' education system combined with the "system of doing business" must have had created a point of no-return for them. This must be regarded as an "inevitable process" in any system of colonisation.

During the initial post-decolonisation decades, perhaps at least until the 1980s, economic development activities were, in general, carried out by the Western world and were based on the assumption that economic development in the developing world would primarily stand for "Westernisation" rather than "modernisation". In fact, attempts at "Westernisation" did not succeed because it failed to achieve the infrastructural bases that the former colonies needed. Furthermore, sufficient emphasis on technical education was not placed in the development process, nor was the need for "capacity building" sufficiently recognised and understood. In 2005, in relation to capacity building in Africa, the Director-General, Operations and Evaluation of the World Bank stated, inter alia, in his Foreword:

> The [World] Bank should reassess what role training should play in its capacity building support, how it should be provided, and what should be the respective roles of a central training unit and regional programmes in any future support for this activity.[14]

In so far as the concepts of "modernisation" and "Westernisation" are concerned the former was really conceptualised and developed by A O Hirchman in his work The Strategy of Economic Development.[15] This concept prompted political scientists, geographers and sociologists to determine the factors of development from a new perspective which was initially experimented in Malaya. But, of course, one of the fundamental papers written on modernisation was by Leinbach[16] who investigated

[14] *Capacity Building in Africa: An OED Evaluation of World Bank Support*, Washington, DC, The World Bank (2005) at IX.

[15] New Haven, Yale University Press (1958).

[16] T R Leinbach, "The Spread of Modernisation in Malaya: 1895–1969" in *Tijdschrift voor Economische en Sociale Geografie* (1972) 262–277.

the modernisation surface in Malaya between 1895 and 1969. Leinbach measured modernisation by referring to the number of hospitals and schools per head of the population, together with indicators such as postal and telegraph facilities, and infrastructural issues namely road and rail facilities. Of the geographers who recognised the importance of the concept, mention should be made of Gould,[17] Hoyle[18] and Safier.[19] Relying on the development process in Tanzania, Lindquist believed in development in phases.[20]

Of course, no discussion of "modernisation" would be complete without referring to Rostow's model of economic growth expressed in his Stages of Economic Growth.[21] Rostow envisaged that there were five stages through which all countries will have to pass in the development process: the traditional society preconditions for take-off—take-off—drive to maturity—the age of high mass consumption. It is in fact a bottom-up approach to development. Incidentally, Rostow, while holding governmental posts in the US, was successful in promoting development policy as US foreign policy.

As to Westernisation, Mehmet[22] confirmed that a Western view, which promoted the idea of science and technology as the tools of development, has become distinctive feature of the principal theories of economic development, whether old or new. The controversies between the concepts of "modernisation" and "Westernisation" are almost never-ending.

[17] P R Gould, "Tanzania, 1920–1963: The Special Impress of the Modernisation Process", 22 *World Politics* (1970) 149–170.

[18] B S Hoyle, "African Socialism and Urban Development: The Relocation of the Tanzanian Capital" in *Tijdschrift voor Economische en Sociale Geografie* (1979) 207–216.

[19] M Safier, "Towards the Definition of Patterns in the Distribution of Economic Development over East Africa", 7 *East Africa Geographic Review* (1969) 1–13.

[20] J Lindquist, "Tanzania: Socialist Ideology, Bureaucratic Reality, and Development from Below" in W B Stöhr and D R Taylor (eds) *Development from Above or Below?* Chichester, John Wiley (1981) 329–349.

[21] W W Rostow, *The Stages of Economic Growth. A Non Communist Manifesto*, Cambridge, Cambridge University Press (1960).

[22] O Mehmet, *Westernizing the Third World*, London, Routledge (1995) and by the same author, *Westernizing the Third World*, second edition, London, Routledge (1999).

In the context of this work, it is to be pointed out however that development must come from within,[23] and for that stage to reach the "process" must be progressive; imitation of others' systems may not work. Development must be achieved through an indigenous process which may be lengthy, but is to be promoted through "capacity building" for which technical assistance from experts may have to be sought. Development must not allow dependency on others. This is what emerging economies and diplomats belonging to the developing world may find useful and worth following.

6.7 Emerging Markets and Diplomacy

It is elementary that an "emerging market" is a market which is "coming up" but not yet fully established in the sense of the established markets in the West. Thus, an emerging market needs nurturing, which would entail forming a strong foundation for it and make provisions for reinforcing that foundation through creativity, sustainable policy-making and implementable strategies.

The strategies of emerging markets, like the established markets should be the same, that is, offensive and defensive, the latter to ensure that its own markets are not unduly overcrowded by foreign enterprises, as otherwise it would amount to creating an economic colonisation. On the other hand, if reciprocity between emerging economies and established economies are not allowed then emerging economies would not be able to pursue an "offensive", aggressive overseas marketing and investment strategy. This is where economic dependency becomes relevant and important.

Economic diplomacy in this context would primarily be achieved by negotiations leading to meaningful bi-lateral treaties of commerce, friendship and investment. The seeking of the right partner(s) is commercially important in this process. However, prior to embarking upon any treaty negotiation, the needs of the country must be clearly identified. The purpose is to acquire knowledge from the more knowledgeable and to create indigenous technology and creativity with the application of that knowledge. In this connection, diplomats may find the UN Report

[23] See further S K Chatterjee, "International Law of Development", 9 *Encyclopaedia of Public International Law, Max Planck Institute for Comparative Public Law and International Law*, 198.

on "Acquisition of Technology"[24] interesting. It is for diplomats to ensure that "as near reciprocity as possible" rather than "dependency" is developed and put that into effect.

The current bi-lateral investment treaties,[25] for example, are not really meant for establishing any real reciprocity between developing countries and developed countries. The treaties concluded particularly since the 1990s bear similar features and contents, and therefore a discussion of these treaties based on three or four samples should reveal the attempts made by investing countries to protect this interest on a non-reciprocal basis between the two contracting parties—an issue of imbalance in protecting the interests of both the parties concerned. Now follows a discussion on the following bi-lateral investment treaties:

(a) Agreement between the Government of Mongolia and the Government of the Kingdom of Denmark concerning the Promotion and Reciprocal Protection of Investments.[26]
(b) Agreement between the Government of the United Kingdom of Great Britain and Northern Ireland and the Government of the Oriental Republic of Uruguay for the Promotion and Protection of Investments.[27]
(c) Agreement between the Government of the Kingdom of Denmark and the Government of the Russian Federation Concerning the Promotion and Reciprocal Protection of Investments.[28]

In so far as the agreement between Denmark and Russia are concerned, whereas a degree of promotion of investment on a reciprocal basis is possible between Denmark and Russia, one may wonder whether any meaningful reciprocal promotion of investment between Denmark and Mongolia may take place (the second agreement cited as an example).

[24] Transnational Corporations in World Development, New York, UN Commission on Transnational Corporations (1988).

[25] Texts of such treaties are available in *UN Treaty Series*.

[26] The text of the treaty has been reproduced in the UN Treaty Series (1998) at 460. This treaty came into force on 2 March 1996.

[27] The text of the treaty has been reproduced in the UN Treaty Series (1998) at 204 This treaty came into force on 1 August 1997.

[28] The text of the treaty has been reproduced in the UN Treaty Series (1998) at 446. This treaty came into force on 25 September 1996.

The same argument may also apply to the treaty between the Government of the United Kingdom and the Government of Uruguay (the third agreement cited as an example). Denmark may not need Mongolia's assistance, technical financial or otherwise, in setting up any industry of similar products, but will be able to exploit natural resources in Mongolia with its attendant benefits. Currently, Uruguay may only be able to service the UK technology in a limited way. In other words, the word "reciprocity" is a misnomer in the context of the purpose of such treaties.

The following are the common clauses in all these treaties, with certain minor variations in them: Definitions, Promotion and Reciprocal Protection of Investments, Treatment of Investments, Expropriation, Compensation for Losses, Transfer of Capital/Payments and Returns, Subrogation, Disputes between an Investor of one Contracting Party and the Other Contracting Party, Disputes between the Contracting Parties and Consultations.

Except the Definition clauses, most of the clauses are meant for the private foreign investor in the host country; these treaties do not contain any clause which would require private foreign investors (transnational corporations) to promote the benefits of host countries by providing them skills, training or any other form of technical assistance, including perhaps, drafting of legislation; unless of course these provisions have been included in a turn-key contract, a reference to which should be made in the main agreement, and the related turn-key contract should be regarded as an integral part of the principal BIT (Bilateral Investment Treaty) otherwise, host countries will experience difficulties in bringing claims in breach of the contract or in contractual negligence against the private foreign investors.

The imbalance in the protection-related provisions is made on the assumption that developing host countries, in practice, withdraw protection from private foreign investors in breach of their treaty obligations. As stated earlier, one should look at this issue from a pragmatic standpoint. During the decolonisation period, it became predictably inevitable that the newly born countries, in their attempts to becoming economically stronger would regain control over and ownership in their natural resources—hence the high incidence of "taking" (nationalisation) of foreign assets, but in most of the cases they paid appropriate[29] compensation to the owner of those assets; but the fear persists, hence the

[29] See UN General Assembly Resolution entitled Permanent Sovereignty over Natural Resources 1962, UNGA Res 1803 (XVII) paragraph 4.

unduly numerous provisions for protection. This issue has been further re-enforced by including the provisions for "fair and equitable treatment" in the Preamble to many BITs. In fact, of the three BITs referred to in this work, save the treaty between the Government of the United Kingdom and the Government of the Oriental Republic of Uruguay, the two other treaties provide for such treatment in the following form:

> Recognising that a fair and equitable treatment of investments on a reciprocal basis will serve this aim. (aim of the BIT)

BIT also include provision for most-favoured nation treatment to be accorded by host countries. A BIT binds a host State in several ways to provide protection to private foreign investors:

(a) the treaty itself which represents a bundle of contractual obligations with the effect of pacta sund servanda;
(b) specific provisions which have already been identified, again with the effect of pacta sund servanda;
(c) fair and equitable treatment—with the binding obligation emanating by virtue of having the effect of pacta sund servanda; the expression, fair and equitable treatment, provokes controversy, but a discussion of it would go beyond the remit of this work;
(d) the principle of State responsibility, which is a compulsory principle of international law and which has formed part of customary international law and
(e) the international minimum standard, which is a compulsory standard of international law, a breach of which gives rise to liability for the violator of the standard.

Based on this discussion it might not be unreasonable to maintain that current BITs fail to strike a balance between the interests of private foreign investors and host developing countries.

One aspect of economic diplomacy is to ensure fairness of benefits out of a deal for both the parties concerned—diplomats may find it worth considering whether the current state practice as evidenced by BITs needs reviewing and more balanced BITs should be concluded. Finally, if private foreign investors are so concerned about the protection of their interests in developing host States, perhaps developing host States through diplomacy should arrange a system whereby under collaborative arrangements between home States and developing host States the causes of apprehension, the lack of appropriate legislation, nationalisation, alleged discriminatory treatment etc. should be dealt with first.

In negotiating such treaties, the issue of "bargaining power" is unduly emphasised. "Bargaining power" stands for the power to "negotiate". There is no room for "muscle power" in negotiating contracts or treaties. It is a game of "brain power" based on a thorough understanding of the issues—each other's needs, and to embody those needs in the form of a document. Of course, such documents will have various dimensions or aspects, namely, objectives, protection of private foreign investors, the emerging investors' protection, mutual favourable treatments in the form of lower tariffs or no tariffs, lower tax on incomes, transmission of profits etc.

An appropriately trained diplomat is a pre-requisite for achieving an effective economic diplomacy. "Effective" in this context would mean "profitable" for the country of the diplomat, which may take the form of "benefit" by virtue of providing skills and training in respect of particular industries, or even technical assistance in any other form, for example, by providing assistance in drafting legislation. An appropriately trained diplomat should be able to understand each other's needs, which in turn, should form the basis for an effective economic rapport.

A diplomat from an emerging economy must appreciate that there might already exist a degree of prejudice against his/her market, and when such prejudice might become evident, he/she must be so trained as to overcome that difficulty, and to establish that the prejudice is not sustainable.

Instead of developing a sense of rivalry between themselves, a diplomat from an emerging market should try to develop and gradually establish rapport so that two apparently opposable parties could work together. Incidentally, from a policy standpoint, as explained earlier, that it might be an idea to work on a BOT or BOOT (Build, Own, Operate and Transfer). Economic diplomacy is a discipline for the best application of which diplomats need to understand not only their needs but also those of the other side with which they may be required to negotiate. In making the foreign policy of a country the issues and matters of economic diplomacy may not be disregarded; in fact, they form an integral aspect of foreign policy-making. In fact, foreign policy-making is often based on the trading interests of the foreign policy-maker.

It is thus essential for emerging markets to strike a balance whereby their own domestic markets would provide a springboard for strengthening their position in chosen overseas markets. Emerging markets are required to be innovative and inventive to be able to compete with the established markets; they may also have to cater for niche markets.

6.8 Conclusions

Emerging markets must remain forward-looking and dynamic. Governmental support for their development is essential. These markets have two major tasks to fulfil: (a) to be able to compete with the established markets; and (b) to improve their domestic markets, which would entail progress and to sustain that progress in all relevant sectors of societies, namely, education, health, industry, employment, agriculture etc. Furthermore, internal development of a country may not be achieved until it has developed a proper democratic process in all aspects of management and governance.

Emerging markets' foreign trade policies and strategies need not be in line with those of the established economies. They should adopt policies which would cater for the needs of the markets on which they have decided to be players. But, when they become active players on the established markets, they will be required to follow the rules and regulations of those markets. In fact, the knowledge they will acquire from those markets, whether from rules and regulations or from mere work practice may be fruitfully utilised in these countries, if appropriate to do so.

Emerging markets are also required to develop confidence in the minds of investors in established markets by means of reliable legislation as a method of risk-minimisation and by operating reliable judiciaries which would be transparent, bias-free and prompt in providing remedies if the interests of private foreign investors are in jeopardy. As stated earlier that in view of the innate apprehension of private foreign investors as to risks prevailing over developing countries, in general, investment flow from developed countries into developing countries decreases. This is one of the reasons why in 1985 the International Bank for Reconstruction and Development (IBRD) established the Multilateral Investment Guarantee Agency (MIGA) [30]

[30] For a basic discussion of MIGA see S K Chatterjee, "The Convention Establishing the Multilateral Investment Guarantee Agency", 36 *International and Comparative Law Quarterly* (1987) 76.

This is not to suggest that all developing countries present judicial risk, and the risks which emanate from the lack of legislation, but it is undeniable that developed countries, in general, perceive so. Whatever might be the reason for their perceiving so, developing countries, in general, and emerging markets, in particular, should take corrective measures to change the perception of developed countries on this matter. In view of their experience in the past, particularly during the colonial and the post-colonial periods (except China of course) emerging markets may also be dynamic enough to present new ideas of investment and development to the world. That knowledge and experience, when appropriately used, would be of immense benefit not only to emerging markets but also to the developed world and particularly for transnational corporations originated in that world.

Non-observance of fundamental rights by emerging markets and developing countries, in general, and even in relation to the rights of employees has become a common ground of criticism against them which has, in effect, adversely affected the investment flow from developed to certain of the developing countries. It is an "issue" which needs to be addressed by them.

It is not by an "accident" that the emerging economies have made their appearance on the world market—it was an inevitability which many countries in the world did not imagine, but economic take-off often takes time. Except China, both Brazil and India went through the experiences of colonisation, but despite their non-participation on the world market in an effective manner since they attained their independence, they have recently realised that capacity building obviously through their technological advancement and skills was essential for them. In the case of China, it is commonly agreed that their governmental and economic policies kept them isolated for a very long time.

Diplomacy for the emergent markets should be dynamic, challenging and mutually understanding but not one of dependency. It should take the form of balancing the interests and commitments of both the emerging markets and the established economies. It should not be diplomacy of "the inferior and the superior" but of equals; its principal aim should be market-creation with a high degree of reciprocity. In order to maintain their effective presence on the world market, emerging markets must remain dynamic, creative and effective participants in international rule-making for matters related to trade and investment.

CHAPTER 7

The Changing Pattern of International Economic Diplomacy

The pace of changes in international economic diplomacy particularly since the 1980s have been rapid. The reasons for this changing pattern of international economic diplomacy are identifiable: (a) the economic aspirations of the newly born countries; (b) empowerment of developing countries derived from their ownership in natural resources; (c) the market domination of the rich particularly consolidated by technological advancement; (d) the rise of regional economic integrations; and (e) a general awareness of economic rights among developing countries, as evidenced by, for example, the UN General Assembly Resolution entitled Permanent Sovereignty over Natural Resources, 1962; the Charter of Economic Rights and Duties of States, 1974 and the Declarations on the New International Economic Order (NIEO), 1974. In fact, the Resolution entitled the Action Plan for a New International Economic Order of 1974 embodied the aspirations of the developing/newly born independent States as to what they would like to achieve through such an economic order.

It has already been stated that international economic diplomacy has a very long history, but in the past, it had certain distinctive features: (a) diplomacy of economic domination[1] as demonstrated during colonisation; (b) such diplomacy between non-colonial powers was primarily

[1] See further C Chatterjee, *International Law and Diplomacy*, London, Routledge (2007) at 129.

C. Chatterjee, *Economic Diplomacy and Foreign Policy-making*,
https://doi.org/10.1007/978-3-030-49047-8_7

of a bi-lateral nature principally to ensure freedom of navigation and commerce, and bi-lateral preferential trade by offering tariff concessions. However, whatever may have been the form of international economic diplomacy in the olden days, the economic reality of demand for and supply of goods combined with the desire to hunt natural resources for the older States to develop commercial friendship with selected States remained. In the olden days, economic diplomacy did not have a truly international dimension; no international economic order was initiated nor was any international economic institution concerned with such an order.

The phenomenon of decolonisation culminating in the self-determination of former colonies into States gradually started giving economic diplomacy a new dimension. They became very conscious of their newly found independence and sovereignty with the human and natural resources, the latter in a large number of the newly born States. This is how the new dynamics of economic diplomacy started particularly since 1974, when the Charter of Economic Rights and Duties of States and the Declaration on the New International Economic Order, 1974 were concluded. Of course, the first glimpse of it may be evidenced in the UN General Assembly Resolution entitled Permanent Sovereignty over Natural Resources, 1962, which offered, inter alia, the guidelines in negotiating terms of private foreign investments in the jurisdictions of developing countries. Their assertion of their newly found sovereignty, and protection of their national interest in inviting private foreign investors were clearly evidenced in this resolution. Contrary to the contemporary practice in concluding investment agreements, provisions for balancing the interests of both private foreign investors and host States should be made. Furthermore, provisions for "buy back"[2] and "capacity building",[3] in particular, should also be incorporated into

[2] "Buy back" is a system which would require a private foreign investor (usually a transnational corporation) to first manufacture quality products meeting the related international standards, and then buy the part of it back in a hard currency to cater for their own domestic markets and even foreign markets, and this way, the indigenous labour force will learn the industry, and the local markets of the host State will have the benefit of high quality products.

[3] "Capacity building" simply stands for enhancing the hands-on experience of the indigenous people, in manufacturing products. This concept may be applied to almost every discipline, including changing of legislations.

such agreements; otherwise, the whole purpose of inviting private foreign investors would be defeated.

Currently, the emerging States, the role of which has been discussed in Chapter 6 of this work, have added a new dimension to economic diplomacy, and their socio-economic prosperity although not comparable as yet with the richest countries in the world, and their onward march in private foreign investment and advancement in technology, in particular, may not be disregarded in developing strategies of economic diplomacy by the developed States. In fact, these emerging markets have already presented business threats to the developed world.

One should not underestimate their capacity to negotiate businesses with foreign partners. Private foreign investors or even foreign parties engaged in any other business including service industries should not begin negotiations with any kind of prejudices against them, including the false perception of "bargaining power". One should also remind oneself of the fact that modern technology is a good source of knowledge and information for them too. Through the internet, they are able to learn what the traditional countries aim and the techniques they, in general, use to achieve their objectives. This is why the role of negotiating techniques assumes importance in economic diplomacy. Trade, investments and security issues being the driving force behind foreign policy-making, diplomats from both developed and developing countries must be familiar with the techniques of negotiating trade and investment contracts. Thus, in a separate chapter of this work,[4] the current weaknesses and gaps in bi-lateral investment agreements have been identified and examined. It is important to bear in mind that in any agreements, particularly of a bi-lateral nature, balancing of interests of both the parties is a vitally important issue.

Based on a bi-lateral investment treaty concluded between two States, when a contract is developed between a transnational corporation (popularly known as multi-national corporation) and a public entity in a host State, then contracts are known as State contracts to which parties are not equal, the public entity in the host State represents its sovereign State, hence it is much stronger in authority than a transnational corporation; after all, a State is a law-making body, and a public entity engaged by the State to apply the law, where necessary. This issue has received attention

[4] Chapter 12.

in a separate chapter of this work,[5] in which the respective responsibilities of both the parties concerned have received attention.

In negotiating a commercial contract or an agreement, the need for both the parties should be borne in mind, rather than basing their negotiations on power or power politics. For historical reasons, many of the developing States still seem to suffer from inferiority complex to a certain extent in negotiating transnational contracts, a discussion of which would be beyond the remit of this work, both the parties (developed and developing) need each other. This statement is equally true of buyers and sellers belonging to the developed and developing worlds. Until developing countries have been assisted by developed countries and their industries to build the requisite capacity of developing countries in the essential areas of economy and education, the latter will remain burdens on the former, and the formal aid-giving, which perhaps has not contributed much to their development process. Incidentally, unless this target has been met, globalisation, may not be achieved either.

Another changing pattern of economic diplomacy emanates from the awareness/consciousness of the developing countries of their sovereignty. Developed countries may not, in reality, regard them as unequal parties; indeed, at negotiation stages, this awareness/consciousness on the part of the developing countries often become evident. They are also conscious of the fact that they have considerable amount of natural resources, in addition to their human resources.

New dimensions to economic diplomacy emerge these days almost on a daily basis, for instance, many may wonder whether bi-lateral "warfares" have anything to do with economic diplomacy; the answer must be in the affirmative. For example, the current Syrian issue is a multi-dimensional one—political, economic, societal, but most of all, a high degree of power game, which has adversely affected not only the indigenous people, but also given rise to transnational terrorism, refugee problem, destruction of infrastructure of the country, which has also resulted in almost a total standstill of the import–export trade to and from the country, to name but a few. Each of these issues has an economic dimension; and a successful diplomatic effort may also resolve these issues otherwise not only the local Syrians will suffer, but also the reconstruction process of the country will prove to be economically burdensome for many other countries.

[5] Chapter 12.

Economic diplomacy, as many will appreciate, is a dynamic discipline an expertise in which requires knowledge in many other disciplines and, in particular, the negotiating techniques including skills in it. A rational economic diplomacy is that diplomacy which by peaceful and friendly means, attempts to protect the national interest in all its forms, but also develops an effective international co-operation, emphasising the real truth; trade and investments between States, are the most effective reasons for remaining friendly with other States. Some of the developing countries have started coming out of their economically dark days; they are now to a large extent occasioning changes in economic diplomacy, and the traditional rich economies are required to pay their attention to those changes. Take, for example, the regional economic integration among several Asian countries known as ASEAN (The Association of South East Asian Nations) which is not as ambitious as the European Union, but economically it is going from strength to strength. In fact, ASEAN may now be treated as a "hub" of private foreign investment.

In negotiating private foreign investment contracts, host developing States, should ensure that while private foreign investors perform their contracts in their jurisdictions, they are required to provide training and skills to the local people (capacity building) for learning the industry; otherwise, economic and skills dependency will persist in the developing world. This issue has also received attention in the chapter entitled State Contracts.

It is to be re-iterated that trade, investment and security issues on a bilateral basis are prime movers of the foreign policy-making of a State. In economic diplomacy, the role of an effective negotiating techniques may not be disregarded bearing in mind that the developing world has also bargaining power; that is, the "power to negotiate." Developing countries are still the principal sources of natural resources; they can easily use that strength as their bargaining chip, but that is precisely what to be avoided in a meaningful and friendly negotiating process. Trade and investment form the basis for inter-State friendship.

Economic diplomacy should be effectively used for achieving international co-operation which unfortunately does not exist in most areas of our life. It should also take a pro-active action for developing binding standards for States in regard to inter-State relationship and make the available international platform (the United Nations) even stronger for developing binding rules of economic relations between States. It is through trade and investment and not by warfares that peace may be brought into the world.

CHAPTER 8

Negotiating Techniques in Economic Diplomacy

8.1 Introduction

Economic diplomacy entails dynamism in the sense in this competitive commercial world diplomats are required not only to be familiar with the latest developments occurring/occurred in regard to any matter or issue coming under the purview of the discipline but also must be innovative and creator of new ideas. It is a difficult task to perform, but it must be performed in that way. It is a discipline which is akin to relationship management which requires good inter-personal skills, in-depth knowledge of the issues/matters, and the capacity to articulate arguments.

Economic diplomacy is also concerned with security issues; if security of a country is in jeopardy so will be the economic sources in that country. This close interrelationship between these two disciplines must not be lost sight of. The legal impact on issues and matters should not be disregarded either. If regional economic unions or associations or blocs, for example, are thought to hinder trade liberalisation, then both politico-economic and legal issues, such as States' rights to enjoy unfettered right to be engaged on a bi-lateral basis with any legitimate regime may not be taken away. Diplomats in support of such causes must have the skills to present these ideas before the World Trade Organization (WTO) or even the UN Conference on Trade and Development (UNCTAD) or any other relevant agencies/offices.

C. Chatterjee, *Economic Diplomacy and Foreign Policy-making*,
https://doi.org/10.1007/978-3-030-49047-8_8

Traditionally, economic diplomacy has predominantly been concerned with private foreign investments, bi-lateral trade (import–export trade), capital markets, socio-economic development, economic migration, employers' rights and environmental issues; but in the contemporary period many other areas, such as security issues, socially unacceptable issues, namely, slave trade, slavery, illicit drug-trafficking, discrimination based on origins of peoples, to name but a few also come under the purview of this discipline. Some of these matters are now discussed.

8.2 Bi-lateral Investments

Bi-lateral investments are usually carried out on the basis of contracts based on bi-lateral investment treaties between two sovereign States. Thus, the contracts are closely developed in accordance with the philosophy of investment enshrined in the corresponding bi-lateral investment treaties. These treaties do not usually balance the interests of the parties; in other words, often they are one-sided treaties; secondly, these treaties are based on the assumption that transnational corporations are vulnerable to the irresponsible behaviour of developing countries, in general, which assumption may not be confirmed. As from the late 1980s hardly foreign assets have been taken in the developing world, and yet after three decades the apprehension still exists in the minds of transnational corporations. This will have a prejudicial impact in drafting such treaties. Take, for example, the Agreement between the Government of Mongolia and the Government of the Kingdom of Denmark concerning the Promotion and Reciprocal Protection of Investments.[1] This may not be regarded as a legal hindrance but the socio-economic philosophies of a country can impact an investment project to which one party belongs to a totally new politico-social and legal environment. This is not to suggest in any way that the socio-economic and legal factors have to be identical between the contracting parties, although evidence exists to confirm that most of the former colonies tend to sign their investment agreements or trade agreements with their former colonies primarily because of similarities in the languages, and legal systems.

[1] UN Treaty Series (1998) at 460. This Agreement came into force on 2 March 1996.

Returning to the Mongolia and Denmark Agreement, it may be pointed out in the form of an introductory comment that the use of the terms "promotion" and "reciprocal protection of investment" in the title of the Agreement should be seriously considered by the lesser party to it. Effectively, the lesser party may not provide "reciprocal protection of investment". Secondly, the Preamble to the Agreement states, inter alia, that:

> Desiring to create favourable conditions for investments in both States and to intensify the co-operation between private enterprises in both States with a view to stimulating the productive use of resources...

The extent to which Mongolia would be able to make investments in the Kingdom of Denmark to the extent the latter may able to do so in Mongolia. Again, the phrase "fair and equitable treatment of investments" has provoked considerable controversy in the world of lawyers.[2] In general, the term is not only vague but also subject to various legal interpretations, a discussion of which would be beyond the context of the main theme of this chapter. Furthermore, it is rather an undue expectation on the part of the investor's country in that "... a fair and equitable treatment of investments on a reciprocal basis..." may be made available by a lesser country to match the standards of the developed country, the other party to the agreement.

These so-called reciprocal agreements contain similar provisions with very few exceptions; for example, definitions, promotion and protection of investments, treatment of investments, exceptions, exemptions, subrogation, dispute between a contracting party and an investor, dispute between the contracting parties, compensation for losses, transfer of capital and returns, consultations etc.

Certain anomalies in such agreement are rather unacceptable, for example, Article 2(2) of the Agreement between:

> Investments of investors of each Contracting Party shall at all times enjoy full protection and security in the territory of the other Contracting Party. Neither Contracting Party shall in any way impair by unreasonable or discriminating measures the management, maintenance, use, enjoyment or

[2] C Schreuer, "Fair and Equitable Treatment in Arbitral Practice", 6 *The Journal of World Investment & Trade*, no 3 (June 2005).

disposal of investments in its territory of investors of the other Contracting Party.

During the negotiation stage, diplomats should make it clear to the other side what objectives they may wish to materialise from such agreements. It is not a lawyer's function to imagine the benefits that both parties to such an agreement may wish to derive from it. Returning to the provisions of Article 2(2) of the Agreement, it is unrealistic to think that a developing country would be able to provide protection to an investment to a level which is usually provided by a developed State. The case in point is *AAPL v the Republic of Sri Lanka*. Furthermore, what is the difference in law between "protection" and "full protection"?

There is no intention to suggest that a host State has no obligation to provide protection to foreign investors and foreign investment. AAPL clearly established that the liability is not of an "absolute nature"; the nature of the liability is "strict"—to make the best efforts to provide protection to foreign investors and investments should do; but the onus is on the host country concerned to establish by evidence that they did their best to provide protection to the foreign party, otherwise host countries concerned under customary international law will be held liable on the grounds of breach of the binding principle of State Responsibility and the international minimum standards, which is a compulsory standard of international law.

These agreements, when examined critically, suggest that the private foreign investors hardly have any obligations towards the host States, not even in respect of the protection of the environment or the obligation to co-operate in the host country's socio-economic development process. These should be incorporated into the underlying treaties, because otherwise, it would be difficult to incorporate them in the corresponding investment contracts.

Article 7 which relates to Transfer of Capital and Returns, requires developing host States to undertake an unduly heavy financial burden on themselves. This is where in-depth negotiations by diplomats would be required. In fact, this statement equally relates to developed countries when they invite investors from other developed States. "Balancing of interest" of both the parties to an agreement is an important issue in negotiating such agreements bearing in mind that reimbursements of remittances of money adversely affects the balance of payments of the country concerned.

The traditional practice of conducting bi-lateral investment treaties between home and host States should be reviewed. Currently, these agreements are almost unilateral in nature. If agreements are to be regarded as bi-lateral, then both parties should "benefit" from them on a balanced basis. The private foreign investors may be asked to train the indigenous people in the industry or industries for which they are being invited by the host State(s); the local people should be given managerial experience too.

Incidentally, "investment" does not necessarily stand for any physical investment in the form of a plant, industry or ventures of a similar nature. Perhaps, the most important form of "investment" would be to develop educational infrastructure, and skills and capacity of human beings. Diplomats engaged in economic diplomacy may find it more satisfying and fulfilling when a country's population will have opportunities to be introduced to education. Education lessens dependency of countries on others.

Investments, in popular perceptions, are meant for making monetary profits; but this perception is not entirely correct; benefits represent the other side of the coin. These benefits are meant for the peoples in host States. This is an important objective of economic diplomacy.

8.3 Trade

It has already been explained that historically bi-lateral trade (often known as international trade but in reality, it is import–export trade) forms the basis for economic diplomacy. In ancient times, trade missions and diplomatic missions were often one and the same.[3] Interestingly enough, these trading activities were primarily operated by representatives of sovereigns, if not, sovereigns themselves, which activities eventually led them to set up consular offices in the sending and receiving States. Trade not only made the two parties inter-dependent but also found the platform for closer friendship. Thus, it may be maintained that trade forms the basis for foreign policy-making. But, of course, in the contemporary period, other issues, namely dependency on defence or security may also contribute to foreign policy-making.

[3] See further Pigman, op. cit., at 139.

Trade in silk and spices, for example, has a very long history dating back to the fifteenth century. This led to the migration of people between the countries of the trading partners; hence arose the need for consular offices in the countries of the trading partners.

Trade required the explorers to explore the sea routes[4] and eventually air routes too. It is to be highlighted that in the absence of any foreign exchange rate system, import–export trade used to be done on "countertrade" basis, which form of trade is still operational. Trade negotiations between countries needed diplomatic skills—economic diplomacy preceded any other form of diplomacy. It is a definitive kind of diplomacy; it requires mastery over negotiating techniques to protect each other's interest, but without hurting the other party, and to do trade on the basis of "trust", bearing in mind that no formal banking system existed until the sixteenth century—but even then, it was in a very rudimentary form. Even today, "trust" remains an important element of inter-State diplomacy.

There exists a concomitant relationship between transport and trade; the former facilitates the latter. Like expansion of transfer network, the protection/security of maritime shipping assumed importance. Both entail very heavy expenditures; thus, in the olden days, only the wealthy countries, be they colonial powers or not were able to actively participate in the shipping and export industries. This is an important issue of economic diplomacy in the contemporary period.

Governments and diplomats of developing countries, in particular, are required to actively participate in "trade facilitation" efforts, such as customs clearance and other administrative barriers. This is where "capacity building" proves to be essential. Seaports and airports should be as mechanised as possible; otherwise trade flow from foreign countries will be adversely affected. This is primarily an internal issue but with the help of external experts this may be achieved. Take, for example, the roll-on and roll-off system at the Djibouti seaports.

Until the mid-twentieth century, bi-lateral trading system developed in a haphazard fashion. Depending upon how close the parties were as business partners, trade concessions and privileges were allowed between themselves. There was no central regulatory body of whatever nature or

[4] Incidentally, three-fourths of world import–export trade are still done through the sea routes.

status until the League of Nations was established in 1919. Article 23, paragraph (e) of the League Covenant provided that:

> ... the Members of the League:
> ... will make provision to secure and maintain freedom of communication and of transit and equitable treatment for the commerce of all Members of the League...

But this was primarily about freedom of communication and of transit, and equitable treatment for the commerce of all Members of the League mainly stood for transit right on an equitable basis for all Members of the League. This is an important aspect of economic diplomacy as without transit right, inter-State trade may not take place. The privilege of transit right also applies to transport of cargo by air, and transport of cargo by road too. But, privilege of this kind was a matter of necessity in the olden days, and could be obtained only by surrendering functional sovereignty by the parties concerned.

In view of this privilege being accorded a customary law status, transit rights are now granted almost automatically, but always on a treaty-basis because transit right is sought to pass through the territorial waters or territorial air space or territorial land space as the case may be. These treaties can be bi-lateral or multilateral in nature. But transit right may not be abused by any beneficiary of it because its purpose is to grant a privilege of an "innocent passage" only; by virtue of it being a privilege, it may be withdrawn by the grantor State at any time but only on valid grounds. In the *SS Wimbledon* case, the Permanent Court of International Justice confirmed the nature of this privilege.[5]

On the other hand, inter-State disputes may arise if the transit passage is not kept safe by the territorial State. In the *Corfu Channel* case[6] two Brutish vessels were destroyed by mines laid in the Channel (Corfu) bed, and the British government brought an action against the Albanian government for failing to provide safe passage through an international channel for the purposes of trade and commerce. The onus was on the Albanian government to prove that it did not lay the mines. According to the International Court of Justice, it was for the coastal State to keep

[5] PCIJ (1923) Series A, No 1.

[6] ICJ Reports (1949) 4.

the territorial waters safe and navigable.[7] There exists an obligation under customary rules of international law for coastal States to provide safe innocent transit passage. The case raised another issue by virtue of the British government's involvement in sweeping the mines in the Albanian territorial waters without the permission of the latter government, which legal issue is beyond the scope of this discussion. This case also signifies the limits of sovereignty as a concept, which should be regarded as a relative concept rather than an absolute concept. A State has an obligation to exercise due care and skill in order to avoid claims based on acts of negligence. Measure of damages will depend on the extent of the negligent act on the part of the negligent State and the causal link between the negligent act, the intention of the negligent party and the extent of damage. As these disputes may be resolved by diplomatic negotiations, diplomats engaged in economic diplomacy should be familiar with these issues rather than initially referring these issues to the legal experts.

Trade is also related to payments. Reduction of tariffs is one thing but in import–export trade, payments to be made by the developing countries in hard currencies[8] to developed countries is a matter for negotiation between the two parties who belong to two different sets of countries. In payment negotiations, it is important to see whether liabilities could be settled in the form of countertrade. This may be construed as the commercial aspect of economic diplomacy.

Countertrade as a method of settling liability has been surrounded by controversies which seem to emanate from prejudice. Of course, when payment is made on countertrade basis, the seller does not receive any money; thus, its foreign exchange reserve does not improve, but the merits of this form of settling dues owed to the other side should be carefully looked into by governments particularly those of developing countries when they acquire technology or expensive products, materials or even an equipment from a foreign country. This can provide positive effect for the country of the provider of goods in the form of increased employment and development of sophisticated skills; on the other hand, the acquiring country would also be required to produce/manufacture as

[7] See further C Chatterjee, *International Law and Diplomacy*, London, Routledge (2007) 286–287.

[8] Currently, the following are the hard currencies: Euro, Russian Roubles, UK Sterling, US Dollars and Japanese Yen.

the case may be, goods of a sophisticated quality whereby it can create employment and its economy becomes skill-based.

As countertrade works between governments or governmental bodies, it is a question of adopting policies and procedures by the governments concerned. Countertrade has a developmental dimension too; as stated earlier that it contributes to capacity building or skills development process. This should be regarded as a socio-economic aspect of economic diplomacy. Thus, a diplomat engaged in economic diplomacy should be familiar with this form of payment and the mechanisms thereof, instead of having any prejudice against it. It is a method of payment which should also work between two developing countries too.

Countertrade stands for trade against trade in goods. It is not a method of payment in the traditional sense of the term, but may be regarded as "consideration" in the English law of contract.[9] There exists a high degree of prejudice against countertrade in general, in that this form of trade is not based on money, thus the sellers would not be able to earn any "hard currencies", but on the other hand, the buyers (particularly developing countries' buyers) can save a considerable amount of hard currencies. Developed countries, such as Australia, New Zealand and the United Kingdom are very much involved in countertrade; in fact, Australia and New Zealand have made countertrade compulsory for offsetting public sector purchases. Whereas Canada, Chile, Kenya or Switzerland, for example, are not in favour of countertrade, Brazil, India, Mexico, South Korea and, in general, Eastern Bloc countries are involved in it. Countertrade has different forms: counterpurchase, barter, buyback etc.,[10] but each form of it are goods-based.

8.4 What Should Be Considered by a Trader Prior to Its Being Engaged in Countertrade?

- The nature of the countertrade policy of the importing country;
- The extent of involvement and performance in countertrade of the importing country;
- The form of countertrade usually adopted by the importing country;

[9] See further C Chatterjee, *Legal Aspects Trade Finance*, London, Routledge (2006) 9.

[10] For other sub-methods of countertrade, see C Chatterjee, *Legal Aspects of Trade Finance*, op. cit., at 12–14.

- The product(s) in which the importing country becomes usually engaged in countertrade;
- The brokers (intermediaries) who are usually involved in countertrade;
- The remedies that may be made available in the event of any breach of the countertrade contract and
- The alternative method(s) of payment which may be offered by the importer's country.

The basic reasons why governments and diplomats may like to choose countertrade:

- To save foreign (hard) currency reserves;
- To provide stimulus for quality production of goods in both the seller's and the buyer's countries and to assure the buyer's country of supplies of quality goods; and
- Development of skills in both buyer's and seller's countries.

8.5 The Most Popular Types of Countertrade

8.5.1 Counterpurchase

In a counterpurchase scheme an exporter purchases goods from the chosen importer's country on condition that the latter is allowed an export contract by the former. There is no reason why counterpurchase scheme may not be applied to services too. Under that scheme two parallel and separate contracts are concluded, one of which is paid for a credit/cash, and the other used on counterpurchase.

In practical terms, under this scheme a developing country imports first and exports later. In this process, the developing importing country earns money by selling the imported goods, and the proceeds of sale helps the importing country to develop products for export to the seller; the importing country is given an opportunity to acquire the material for the "to be exported goods" on a loan basis. It is to be noted however that counterpurchase obligations may be assigned to third parties, and in that event the latter will undertake the same obligations as one of the original parties and will have the right to deal directly with the other countertrade partner.

Counterpurchases may be either mandatory or non-mandatory; whereas Indonesia, for example, prefers mandatory counterpurchases; India and Malaysia prefer the non-mandatory form. But whether the form is mandatory or non-mandatory, the parties concerned usually enter a clause to that effect in the tender documents. Incidentally, in certain cases, counterpurchase may require some payment of money.

8.5.2 *Barter*

Under this scheme also goods and services are exchanged for goods and services. Instead of any parallel contracts as in the case of countertrade, a single contract is concluded. Goods are imported first, and goods for the buyer will be exported after the imported goods have been sold. The basis of barter trade is "trust" between the two parties concerned. Under a barter arrangement, the parties (the governments/government departments) have a considerable degree of flexibility in determining the terms and conditions of their contracts. However, if a developing country imports first, usually a condition is incorporated into the agreement whereby it will be required to settle the liability as soon as the imported goods are sold, and the goods are exported thereafter without delay.

8.5.3 *Buy-Back*

The buy-back system entails transfer of capital or equipment in order to activate it. Under this system, the acquirer of the capital or equipment would be involved in manufacturing a pre-determined quantity of product in a pre-determined currency in order to settle the debt occasioned by the acquisition of the capital or equipment. The provider of the capital or equipment becomes the first buyer for the acquirer of technology. Thus, that buyer can acquire high quality products at a low price for its own domestic market or even foreign markets. This spreads the name of the manufacturers of products too.

It is usual to supplement buy-back arrangements with Turn-Key Contract, which may be described as skills development contract, whereby after appropriate training (skills development) the beneficiaries are able to turn the key to the industry concerned. A turn-key contract will have two distinct features: (a) "product in-hand"—what is meant by the phrase is that based on the training and skills gained, the local workers have been able to develop high quality products, which should be regarded as an achievement and (b) "market hand" which would mean that with the help of the foreign contractor/company the host State or their company has also explored markets for their products; however, the first buyer would be foreign company/contractor, and that they will "buy-back" good quality products at a low price. Thus, both the parties benefit from such arrangements.

However, there are certain risks usually associated with the buy-back arrangement:

- Unless the buy-back price has been pre-fixed, it may be subject to currency fluctuations leading to financial losses;
- In the event of the gap between the time of contracting and the time of manufacturing being considerable, significant fluctuations in price may take place.

These risks may be avoided by making "prompt delivery" a term of the contract. In fact, the advantages of the buy-back system seem to outweigh its disadvantages. As stated earlier that under this arrangement both parties benefit, one monetarily and the other qualitatively—by gaining new training and skills. Incidentally, the earned training and skills will also be helpful for satisfying the demands of the domestic market for those products.

This is a method of settling liabilities which requires good negotiating techniques and which diplomats engaged in commercial/economic diplomacy must possess and use effectively. This type of commercial/economic diplomacy strengthens the platform for further rapport—commercial/economic diplomacy in this way leads its way to foreign policy-making.

The right to trade (import–export) should be available to every State in the world, but this right may be taken away or limited or restricted by two specific ways: (a) by imposing sanctions on a country with which friendly relations between the two States have been strained leading to cessation of diplomatic relations between them or that it has been subject to the UN sanctions and (b) by restricting or effectively denying "market access" to countries which are not members of an economic union or area.

8.6 Conclusions

A diplomat engaged in economic diplomacy should continue negotiating economic deals in the broadest sense of the term, because it is this form of diplomacy that keeps general diplomacy alive and interesting. But, economic diplomacy cannot be a form of diplomacy of dominance which happened in recent years, by and through large amounts of aid or supply of weapons or by some other means which, in reality, amounts to corrupting the minds of recipients of favours.

CHAPTER 9

Economic Diplomacy in Crisis

9.1 Introduction

The objectives of economic diplomacy have already been discussed in Chapter 1 of this work. Depending upon the nature of the scope of the economic diplomacy, these objectives may be achieved either by bi-lateral or multilateral initiatives which would culminate in bi-lateral or multilateral treaties. It is to be emphasised however that examples of successful multilateral co-operation are rather few, but nevertheless, given the nature of contemporary crises, political, economic and security-related issues, in particular, economic diplomacy, if not conducted with the constraints placed on it, will not succeed. To what extent has the firmament of economic diplomacy changed and what must be done to develop new diplomatic practice to cope with the demands of this new phenomenon?

At the outset, one should comprehend the complexities of the new environment which would necessitate engaging in new rules of diplomacy with a wider perspective capable of dealing with truly international or transboundary issues and problems. Multifarious reasons are responsible for the causation of this new phenomenon, namely, a much wider division of the world between the "haves" and the "have-nots", political and economic aspirations of the people in both the rich and the poor parts of the world, transnational terrorism endangering lives and security of people, environmental issues, war-ridden communities giving rise to the migration of people, an issue requiring an urgent attention of

C. Chatterjee, *Economic Diplomacy and Foreign Policy-making*,
https://doi.org/10.1007/978-3-030-49047-8_9

the international community, ever-increasing problems related to politico-economic self-determination, creating new problems by controlling the supply of basic commodities by the primary commodity producing countries, technology-related problems including cybercrimes and even piracy on the sea, to name but a few.

It is the purpose of this chapter to justify why new rules, an informed and a dynamic nature of economic diplomacy has proved to be essential in the contemporary world.

9.2 Analysing the Correlation Between the New Issues and the Need for an Informed and Dynamic Nature of Economic Diplomacy

Historically, economic diplomacy preceded the so-called political economy; it has been emphasised in this work that economic issues, such as import–export trade, private foreign investment largely shape the foreign policy of a State. Granted that over the past decades security issues have also drawn the attention of diplomats and foreign offices in developing their foreign policies, but this practice should be reviewed. Maintenance of the national security is imperative for any State, but over-charging of foreign policies with an undue emphasis on security issues is to be regarded as an unusual dimension to foreign policy-making, the primary objective of which is to develop friendly relations between States. The causes giving rise to world-wide terrorism or trans-border immigration or cybercrimes etc., for example, should be carefully looked into, rather than heightening the need for giving special emphasis to security issues in foreign policies defeats the whole purpose of foreign policy-making, the primary objective of which is to develop friendly relations among States.

There is no need to detail the causal connection between the issues stated above and their consequential effect in this context; suffice to mention that no State, powerful or weak, should contribute to such issues, because their effect adversely affects every State and de-stabilises the whole political systems of countries. Furthermore, any measures, preventative or curative, costs States money, and the poorer States will be required to meet these expenses usually on borrowed money or aid, which, in turn, would precipitate economic dependency on lenders or aid providers as the case may be. Some of the principal causes of unpredictability in economic diplomacy seem to have been caused by the following: new aspirations of the newly born States in regard to their economic self-sufficiency and socio-economic development which became evident first in 1960s[1] and then again in the 1970s,[2] although a critical analyst might say that it really started with the coming into force of the UN Charter. Of course, the UN General Assembly Resolution on the Granting of Independence to Colonial Countries and Peoples, 1960, embodied the essence of economic self-determination too. The relevant provision in the 1960 Resolution provided that:

> All peoples have the right to self-determination; by virtue of that right they freely determine their political status and freely pursue their economic, social and cultural development.

Between 1974 and the following UN General Assembly Resolutions which were initiated by developing countries are worth mentioning. Then came the Rio Declaration of 1992, Principle 13 of which provides that:

> States shall develop national law regarding liability and compensation for the victims of pollution and other environmental damage. States shall also co-operate in an expeditious and determined manner to develop further international law regarding liability and compensation for adverse effects of environmental damage caused by industries within their jurisdiction or control to areas beyond their jurisdiction.

The concept of the Exclusive Economic Zone which has been incorporated into the UN Convention on the Law of the Sea (UNCLOS III) 1982 was initiated by Dr F Nzenga, then a Kenyan Minister, and which is now followed by all States, developed and developing. The Doha Declaration of 2002 and 2005 also clearly identified the socio-economic aspirations of developing countries. Finally, The Addis Ababa Action Agenda entitled Financing for Development, 2015 is also worth mentioning. These are some of the examples of the documents in which the socio-economic aspirations of developing countries, in general, have

[1] The UNGA Resolution entitled Permanent Sovereignty over Natural Resources, 1962, UNGA Res 1813.

[2] The New International Economic Order 1974, and the Charter of Economic Rights and Duties of States, 1974.

become evident. In negotiating bi-lateral treaties or multilateral treaties or bi-lateral contracts of an economic dimension, parties to these instruments, irrespective of economic or military or political status should bear these aspirations in mind and negotiations of these instruments should be carried out accordingly. Developing countries, on the other hand, should also appreciate that all instruments must be based on mutual benefit.

The causes of differences between parties, usually States, must be thoroughly studied for they eventually lead to small to large warfares. These differences often arise owing to prejudices against another group or groups of people or owing to historical misconception or for denial of the truth of the courses of the differences of ideas and perceptions between the parties concerned. Incidentally, perhaps there is a tendency to call these differences "conflicts"; which may not be a correct expression. Differences of ideas or perceptions over issues usually lead to warfares, which should be avoided, as no party benefits from it; the innocent people and children for example get killed, and economic devastations and migration of people take place. Examples of such warfares based on differences in perceptions of ideologies or prejudices are available.

On the other hand, during the decolonisation period, primarily between 1945–1984, the act of taking control over their natural resources (from the companies or other legal entities of the colonial powers) was severely criticised by many of the colonial powers, without appreciating that all States would like to have not only ownership over their natural resources but also control over them. This has been the norm, in general, in the developed world too.[3] But, in the vast majority of cases, appropriate compensation in the agreed currency has been paid for by the newly independent States in accordance with the provisions of paragraph 4 of the UNGA Resolution entitled Permanent Sovereignty over Natural Resources, 1962.[4] The issue of taking of assets by the newly born States, in their attempts to secure economic independence, received a mixed reception in the hands of academics.[5] Incidentally, it is interesting to point out that the majority of the Bi-lateral Investment Treaties still provide for

[3] See K Katzarov, *Theory of Nationalisation*, The Netherlands, Springer (1964).

[4] Op. cit.

[5] See, for example, B Wortley, *Expropriation in Public International Law*, Cambridge, Cambridge University Press (1959); G White, *Nationalisation of Foreign Property*, London, Stevens (1961); C Chatterjee, *International Law and Diplomacy* (2011), op. cit.

"adequate compensation" in the event of taking of any assets of private foreign investors by host States. This is a matter which deserves a serious attention of diplomats engaged in economic diplomacy. The causes of the differences of opinion between the former colonial powers and the newly independent States were clear.

But, of course, acts of illegal taking of private foreign assets would not attract any sympathy from any corner.[6]

Another example of misconception which often gives rise to economic discrimination between trading partners under the same treaty is the operation of the Most-Favoured Nation Treatment through the MFN clause, which has a very long history,[7] but no action is being taken by promoters of economic diplomacy. The economic circumstances in which the Most-Favoured Nation Treatment originated in the history of transnational trade during the fifteenth century, are irrelevant in the contemporary world. It does not create "equality in fact" between the trading partners to a multilateral trade treaty. In 1941, the US Trade Department pointed out the limitations of the MFN preference when it stated that:

> It is to be admitted that the most-favoured nation principle alone, without a moderate level of non-discriminatory rates, is not sufficient of itself to promote a healthy international trade. The United States has since recognized this fact I the enactment of the Trade Agreement Act.[8]

According to Schwarzenberger:

> It [MFN] serves increasingly to provide proportional, rather than absolute equality between the beneficiaries.[9]

[6] See for example, "BP-Libya", 53 *International Law Reports* 297, "Texaco-Libya", 17 *International Legal Materials* (1978) 1 and "Liamco-Libya Arbitrations", 20 *International Legal Materials* (1981) 1; see also LETCO Arbitration ICSID Case No ARB/83/2.

[7] Memorandum of the Chief of the Division of Commercial Treaties and Agreements (Hawkins) to Assistance Secretary of State, Acheson, 1 August 1941, *Foreign Relations*, vol. III, 19–21.

[8] See Footnote 7.

[9] G Schwarzenberger, "The Principles and Standards of International Economic Law", 117 *Recueil des Cours*, The Hague Academy of International Law (1966) I, 1–98 at 77; see also by the same author, "The Most-favoured Nation Standard in British Practice", 22 *British Year Book of International Law* (1945) 96–121 at 96; S K Hornbeck, "The

The causes of discrimination between trading partners are not being closely scrutinised by advocates of multilateral trading arrangements. By the same token, the economic impact of regional trading arrangements on the economies of non-member States, some of which are now regarded as emerging markets having obtained the capacity and skills of manufacturing high quality products, as well as some of the developing countries, certain selected products of which have traditionally met the international and Western States' standards and indeed competitive in price, are being denied free market access by these regional bodies. These issues cause tension between States, members of the international community, for non-friendly treatment and discriminatory treatment between States. In the final analysis, this kind of discriminatory treatment disturbs the world economic order or disturbs the formation of such an order. Again, this was one of the reason for adopting the Resolution on a New International Order, 1974 although some of its provisions need reviewing.

The contemporary rules of power politics need to be reviewed. It is not by warfares that differences between States or between States and factions may be resolved. The current world has been torn with warfares since 1962 (the Vietnam War) but no war has ended in a clear success, human miseries and pollution of the environment, killings of people, de-stabilisation of political regimes and economies, and displacement of people, have remained rampant. This directly impacts upon the process of economic diplomacy in that owing to warfares, economies and the people therein become victims in consequence of which governmental plans for socio-economic development process are disturbed; many victim countries will be burdened with aid or financial assistance the ultimate result of which would be financial dependency on the donors, a situation which requires time to overcome; and most of the efforts in relation to economic diplomacy will be required to be diverted from aid-seeking unless the country has insufficient funds to meet the additional expenditures. Furthermore, warfares usually require majority of the countries to buy weapons from other countries; never-ending miseries of all kinds. Thus, it is essential for diplomats to acquire special skills to negotiate all differences between the parties concerned. In fact, there is a duty for diplomats to negotiate.

Most-favoured Nation Clause" (Part I) 3 *American Journal of International Law* (1909) 395–422; S K Chatterjee, "Forty Years of International Action for Trade Liberalization", 23 *Journal of World Trade* (1989), op. cit., at 45.

9.3 The Qualities of a Good Negotiator in Economic Diplomacy

Negotiations are a two-way process, which should not be started with any pre-conceived ideas. In fact, many people still believe that non-Western countries lack knowledge, and that the former has domineering bargaining power, which belief is totally wrong. "Bargaining power" does not stand for "muscle power" or "financial power"; it simply stands for the power to negotiate. Negotiation is a face-to-face interaction between people. Both parties aim at earning as much benefits as possible through negotiations—but they must be prepared for "mutual benefit"; otherwise, the purposes of negotiations are defeated. What to negotiate must be determined beforehand with alternative strategies.

In order to successfully negotiate, a diplomat must have a thorough knowledge in the subject matter of negotiation. In the case of economic diplomacy, the economic benefits that both the parties may derive from a deal must be thought through prior to coming to the negotiation table. Economic diplomacy's function is not to deepen economic dependency, rather it should attempt to emancipate a country from it. Take, for example, transfer of technology, which has proved to be a common phenomenon between developed and developing countries; however, based on the practice of developing countries, in general, it may be stated that technology transfer from developed to developing countries generally has been what may be described as a "one-way traffic". This is so because developing countries tend to perceive transfer of technology (which is, in reality, transfer of knowledge) a kind of favour they are seeking from the transferor. This may be described as a direct effect of "colonialism"—a submissive behaviour rather than treating them as "equals". In this connection, two documents should be referred to which both parties, the transferor and the transferee, may find useful:

(a) the Report on Acquisition of Technology developed by the Committee on Transnational Corporations incorporated into the publication entitled Transnational Corporations in World Development. Although quite an old document, it is believed that its contents are, in the main, still relevant[10] and

[10] See Transnational Corporations in World Development 1990.

(b) the Draft Code of Conduct on Transfer of Technology developed by UNCTAD in 1985.

The first Report clearly recommended, inter alia, that ideally, technology should be "indigenous" and "according to the needs" of the country concerned. The advantages of this recommendation are obvious; furthermore, this process would contribute to what is known as capacity building; it also clearly identified the strategies of technology acquisition in the following passage:

> ... that an indigenous technological capability is a necessary condition for the evaluation of technology to be obtained from abroad, for the effective utilisation of the transferred technology, for the adaptation to local conditions for getting better terms for the transfer in negotiations with foreign enterprises and for the generation of "appropriate" indigenous technologies. In other words, indigenous technological capability is not an alternative to transfer but a necessary condition for it.[11]

It also emphasises that the price of technology is determined through sheer "bargaining power", as technology market is imperfect and there does not exist any catalogue of prices. This point becomes particularly important when countries acquire "old" technology. If a country plans to strengthen her position as a technology and knowledge-based economy, then diplomats should negotiate technology acquisition to their best interest which may be achieved through the "buy-back" system, which is still neglected by the vast majority of countries in the world. The "buy-back" system is now explained in the following way:

9.3.1 Stage I

Country A owns the most appropriate type of technology for Country B	Country B plans to acquire Country A's technology

[11] Op. cit., at 50.

9.3.2 *Stage II*

The Negotiation Stage

Country B identifies the benefits that Country A may derive from transfer of technology and setting up a manufacturing business in Country B, for example, cheaper labour force, cheaper materials, low tax level, protection of the industry etc., but in the negotiation process B must enter the condition of "capacity building" (training for indigenous people in that production process). Price must be determined by referring to the benefits that Country A would derive from this deal. The issue of acquiring equity ownership in the company by B's people should also be negotiated at this stage

---

9.3.3 *Stage III*

The Installation of the Technology and Production Processes

At this stage Country A's engineers and experts must teach the techniques of manufacturing the product (capacity building) and allow participation of B's people in the management of the industry. A will thus manufacture high quality product at a low cost of production; B will have capacity building whereby its own people will learn how to manufacture that product and to gain industry self-sufficiency

---

9.3.4 *Stage IV*

Buy-back Stage

It will be a term of the contract whereby Country A will be required to buy-back part of that product in a mutually chosen hard currency to cater for her own domestic market, and to find export markets for Country B and/or for Country A too. The net result will be that B will learn how to manufacture a quality product, which she would be able to export, while A will be able to expand her markets by virtue of manufacturing a quality product at a very competitive cost

---

The UNCTAD Code of Conduct simply emphasises the objectives of technology transfer and identifies the clauses that should not be incorporated into a transfer of technology contract. It is to be re-iterated that the attainment of economic independence is one of the core objectives of economic diplomacy, which, in turn, would foster friendly relations between States.

Returning to the issue of negotiating techniques, it is worth mentioning that negotiators, be they diplomats or otherwise, must have the following qualifications: calm, bias/prejudice free, open-minded, very good familiarity with the causes of the difference, if any, between the parties concerned, or the commercial matter in connection with which negotiation will be undertaken with the other side. Both the parties should be on an equal footing, as the concept of "bargaining power" which prevails in the minds of many is misconceived. Of course, this bargaining power will be compromised when one party has already been benefited by the other whether by virtue of receiving aid or loan or otherwise. In other words, economic or financial dependency or even military dependency directly affects the bargaining position of the other recipient negotiation party, which has often been the case.

The primary objective of an effective negotiation is to achieve benefits for both the parties. In the example given above, setting up of industries in a receiving State by a corporation of a sending State will benefit both the parties. It is repeated if the result of negotiation benefits only one side then it is not negotiation, it is simply an imposition of the terms of the stronger on to the weaker, and to achieve that end, there is no need for engaging oneself in a so-called negotiation process.

Missions particularly from the developing countries located in the rich receiving countries, namely, Australia, Canada, Denmark, France, Germany, Japan, the Netherlands, Sweden, the UK and the US, in particular, should really bear in mind the importance of capacity building rather than weakening their position as borrowers.

9.4 Conclusions

There is no room for application of any doctrinal concepts in economic diplomacy. It is a form of diplomacy which is almost solely concerned with beneficial deals to be struck between a receiving State's economic entities and a sending State, in relation to developing principles and standards of economic diplomacy between States.

It has already been pointed out that the principal function of negotiations on economic issues on a bi-lateral basis is to build capacity of a country, particularly a developing country by learning skills and acquiring knowledge in order to ensure that eventually with governmental assistance, the country will become innovative and inventive in due course.

In strengthening the processes of economic diplomacy, international co-operation would be essential, which is currently almost non-existent. Perhaps States should start diplomatic negotiations at bi-lateral and regional levels first; the platforms of international organisations, such as the UN, WTO, ILO and the IMF etc. as the case may be would be essential for developing guidelines of conduct on various issues which really relate to the international community, namely, slave trade, slavery, economic terrorism, environmental issues etc.

In economic diplomacy, the tendency to use sovereignty in its absolute form by the members of the international community needs to be restricted and used only in very exceptional cases on justifiable grounds, bearing in mind that the excuse of the national interest is often abused by States. The incidence of economic crisis is often heightened by States owing to the lack of understanding that economic diplomacy entails accommodation of the aspirations of States with which the traditional economic diplomacy does seem to have been deeply concerned.

CHAPTER 10

International Trade Practice

10.1 Introduction

Institutionalisation of trade practice would stand for that practice which has been adopted by the international community and has led to the development of customary international law—the practice-based law. Evidence of such law may be found in the form of trade practice, for example, the documentary credit mechanism or the bills of exchange or bills of lading. These may be described as transactional tools of import–export trade, but it is for the trading partners and their diplomats to develop more framework regulations to standardise trade practice.

10.2 A Brief Analysis of the Growth and Development of the Internationalisation of Trade

Many trade practices have a long history; the process of institutionalisation of trade practice and policies formally started with the League of Nations. Article 23(e) of the League Covenant provided that:

> … the Members of the League … will make provision to secure and maintain freedom of communication and of transit and equitable treatment for the commerce of all Members of the League. In this connection, the special necessities of the regions devastated during the war of 1914-1918 shall be borne in mind.

C. Chatterjee, *Economic Diplomacy and Foreign Policy-making*,
https://doi.org/10.1007/978-3-030-49047-8_10

The League's effort to institutionalise trade or to develop a framework convention addressed to all Members was rudimentary or at the most inadequate. The League was more concerned with issues relating to warfare, rights of minorities, mandated territories, etc.

The UN, on the other hand, made it clear through its Charter that socio-economic co-operation can form the foundation of peace; and that warfare or use of force must be abolished. Unfortunately, both the objectives of the founders of the UN have failed. However, it is still possible to transform the failure to a success provided, of course, its Member States reflect on the objectives of the UN.

The socio-economic objectives of the UN were rather extensively pervasive. It institutionalised its objectives by establishing the Economic and Social Council (ECOSOC) with a very comprehensive mandate. The success record of the Economic and Social Council is quite impressive. Based on its mandate which is shown below, it has developed a very large number of international conventions and resolutions particularly in relation to the issue of socio-economic development in the international community. Article 12 of the UN Charter provides that:

> 1. The Economic and Social Council may make or initiate studies and reports with respect to international economic, social, cultural, educational, health and related matters and may make recommendations with respect to any such matters to the General Assembly of the United Nations and to the specialized agencies concerned.
> 2. It may make recommendations for the purpose of promoting respect for, and observance of, human rights and fundamental freedoms for all.
> 3. It may prepare draft conventions for submission to the General Assembly, with respect to matters falling within its competence.

Chapter IX of the UN Charter entitled "economic and social cooperation", is also worth looking at. Articles 55 and 56, falling under this Chapter provide that:

> Article 55
>
> With a view to the creation of conditions of stability and well-being which are necessary for peaceful and friendly relations among nations based on respect for the principle of equal rights and self-determination of peoples, the United Nations shall promote:

a. higher standards of living, full employment, and conditions of economic and social progress and development;
b. solutions of international economic, social, health and related problems, and international cultural, educational co-operation; and
c. universal respect for, and observance of, human rights and fundamental freedoms for all without distinction as to race, sex, language or religion.

It is elementary but nevertheless important to emphasise that trade and investment, domestic and foreign, initiated by a country forms the basis for social well-being of the peoples belonging to a country. This is one of the most important links between trade and investment and socio-economic development; there of course remain other links too, namely stability and predictability of policy-making, education, health, etc., trade and investments at a non-domestic level by partners promotes and consolidates bi-lateral friendship—an act of diplomacy; they also form the bases for peaceful and friendly relations among States, and in Chapter IX (Article 55) of the UN Charter, the UN programmes for achieving socio-economic and means thereof have been detailed.

Indeed, through Article 56 of the UN Charter, all Members of it pledged themselves

> ... to take joint and separate action in co-operation with the Organization for the achievement of the purposes set for in Article 55.

The word "pledge" has a "contractual" essence; a promise which the Member States voluntarily undertook to perform. Have the Member States honoured their "pledge"; alternatively, have there been any proactive diplomacy initiated by the Member States of the UN? This may be considered from three points of view: (a) either the Member States are indifferent to what the UN plans to do; or (b) they are not familiar with the UN activities and do not want to be familiar with them or (c) they do not want to accept the recommendations made by the ECOSOC or the General Assembly on the rather irrational perception that "recommendations" are not legally binding. Legally speaking, the Member States should have reflected on this last issue before they undertook that "pledge" under Article 56. The net result is that almost nothing has been achieved.

As to the perception that recommendations of the General Assembly or ECOSOC are not binding, many authors have already expressed a variety of views, mainly suggesting that they may at most be treated as a source of "soft law". This issue has received attention in a separate section of this chapter.

10.3 A Critical Examination of the MFN System

Returning to the issue of "institutionalisation" of trade protection, it should be pointed out that "preferential trading systems" have had a very long history whereby States on a bi-lateral basis primarily for historical reasons offered such arrangements with a view to consolidating their position as friendly trading partners. In this practice, there was no need for justifying the reason for according such privileges—a prerogative of sovereign States. But there came changes—the trading world wanted "commercial equality" whereby preferences accorded to a second party should be made available to all the third parties belonging to a treaty, that is, preferential arrangements accorded by means of bi-lateral arrangements (treaties) should provide for privileges to third parties belonging to the same treaties—the origins of the Most-Favoured Nation clause. Under this arrangement whatever preferences (mainly in the form of tariff reductions in relation to trade) may have been accorded to a third party; the second party (the most-favoured nation) and other parties to the treaty will automatically be entitled to the privilege based on the notion of commercial equality. Although it apparently seems to create commercial equality in law, it may not create equality in fact.

The foundation of trade liberalisation and commercial equality under the pre-GATT, during the GATT period and post-GATT (WTO period) period has been based on the traditional concept of the Most-Favoured Nation (MFN) standard (which is not yet a compulsory standard of international economic law) which was embodied in Article 1 of the General Agreement on Tariffs and Trade (GATT) and what was the rationale behind the MFN standard and why do trade treaties still incorporate them? The historical practice and experience formed the basis for this standard. According to Schwarzenberger:

> … the principles of MFN and national treatment made their first appearance in international law proper in the commercial treaties concluded

> during the twelfth century between English and Commercial powers and cities.[1]

Hornbeck however maintained that the standard of the Most-Favoured Nation first appeared in commercial treaties towards the close of the seventeenth century.[2] It has been a matter of practice for the commercial world to incorporate this standard in their trade and investment treaties.[3] According to Hornbeck again:

> During the nineteenth century, while international trade became world commerce, commercial treaties became so common that they now bind the trading nations in a fine-meshed web. In these treaties the clause of the most-favoured nation was inserted with so few exceptions as to warrant its characterization as the cornerstone of all modern commercial treaties.[4]

The Economic and Financial Committee of the League of Nations also realised that a discriminatory trade policy would also adversely affect the prospect of world peace.[5] This view of the League, albeit a defunct institution, is, in principle, still true. Peace may be brought through non-discriminatory trade and investment policies, among other measures—a policy-hint for diplomats.

The Havana Charter which, incidentally, to a certain extent formulated some of the principles of GATT, also advocated the operation of the MFN treatment as a means of avoiding discriminatory treatment in cross-border trade.[6] Despite its limitations, MFN clauses were, as a matter of practice, included in trade treaties apparently for two obvious reasons: (a) that it became customary to do so without questioning its shortcomings; and (b) that this standard was the only popular standard perceived to be a tool to attain commercial equality. This standard attained so much popularity

[1] G Schwarzenberger, "The Most-Favoured Nation Standard in British State Practice", 22 *British Year Book of International Law* (1945) 96–121 at 96.

[2] S K Hornbeck, "The Most-Favoured Nation Clause (Part 1)", 3 *American Journal of International Law* (1909) 395–422 at 395.

[3] See Appendix to this work.

[4] Ibid.

[5] League of Nations, Commercial Policy in the Inter-War Period: International Proposals and National Policies (1942) at 47–51.

[6] See further C A Wilcox, *A Charter for World Trade*, New York, Macmillan (1949).

that it was extended to include matters, such as importation, exportation, transit rights, customs duties, tariffs, etc.[7] Based on treaty practice it would be possible to maintain that this preference may take the following main forms: (a) conditional; (b) unconditional; (c) unilateral; (d) reciprocal; (e) absolute and (f) relative. Each of these forms is self-explanatory. Under this scheme a preference is usually offered on a product-by-product or service-by-service basis. The question remains whether tariff preferences based on the MFN Standard may create "equality in fact".

Schwarzenberger pointed out that:

> It serves increasingly to provide proportional, rather than absolute equality between the beneficiaries.[8]

The scope of MFN treatment also varies considerably depending upon the needs and policies of the States applying it. According to Schwarzenberger again:

> Though the principle of reciprocity affords a certain amount of protection to small States, they may challenge the limitations imposed on the MFN standard by the greater powers only at the risk of being excluded from the benefits of the standard in extensive areas of the world.[9]

By virtue of not being part of customary international law, any automatic application of the MFN system by any State may not be assumed. In 1941, the US Department of State identified the limitation of the MFN preference in the following passage:

> It is to be admitted that the most-favoured nation principle alone, without a moderate level of non-discriminatory rates, is not sufficient of itself

[7] For a discussion of the need for a wider application of the most-favoured nation standard, see the *Report of the International Law Commission* (1969) vol. II, UN Doc. A/CN.4/213.

[8] G Schwarzenberger, "The Principles and Standards of International Economic Law", 7 *Recueil des Cours* The Hague Academy of International Law (1966) I, 1–98 at 77.

[9] G Schwarzenberger, The Most-Favoured Nation Standard in British Practice", op. cit., at 106.

to promote a healthy international trade. The United States has since recognised this fact in the enactment of the Trade Agreement Act.[10]

"Equality in law" rather than "equality in fact" may not achieve any genuine equality. The case in which this issue was considered by the Permanent Court of International Justice was the Minority Schools in Albania.[11] Sometime in December 1920, the Assembly of the League of Nations recommended that in the event of Albania becoming a Member of the League, she would be required to enforce the principles of the Minorities Treaties. On 2 October 1921, Albania signed a Declaration, Article 5, paragraph (4) of which provided, inter alia, that:

> Albanian nationals who belong to racial, religious, or linguistic minorities will enjoy the same treatment and security in law and in fact as other Albanian nationals. In particular they shall have an equal right to maintain, manage and control at their own expense or to establish in the future, charitable, religious and social institutions, with the right to use their own language and to exercise their religion freely therein.

However, in 1993, the State's National Assembly amended Articles 206 and 207 of the Albanian Constitution of 1928 in the following way:

> The instruction and education of Albanian subjects are reserved to the state and will be given in the State's schools. Primary education is compulsory for all Albanian nationals and will be given free of charge. Private schools of all categories at present in operation will be closed.

The consequences of this provision were clear: all private schools for all the minorities, including those of the Greek minorities were closed down. This was an act of equality in law, but not in fact, and this analogy may be drawn with the trade-related issues too. The Spanish representative took the initiative to prompt the League Council to seek an Advisory Opinion from the Court on whether the Albanian Government's act whereby the minorities in Albania would be treated on an equal basis

[10] Memorandum of the Chief of the Division of Commercial Treaties and Agreements (Hawkins) to Assistant Secretary of State, Acheson, 1 August 1941, Foreign Relations, vol. III, 19–21 Ct. M. Whiteman, 14 *Digest of International Law*, op. cit., at 749.

[11] PCIJ (1935) Series A/B No. 64.

with the majority in contravention of the relevant provisions of the Declaration of 2 October 1921, and also contrary to the letter and spirit of the stipulations laid down in Article 5, paragraph 1 of the Declaration.

In its Defence, the Greek Government stated in its submission, inter alia, that:

> ... the fundamental idea of Article 5 of the Declaration was on the contrary to guarantee freedom of education to the minorities by guaranteeing them the right to retain their existing schools and to abolish others, if they desired...[12]

In providing the meaning of the phrase "the same treatment and security in law and in fact" which was embodied in the League Council's Resolution of 18 January 1935, the Court stated that:

> ... the same treatment and security in law and in fact implies a notion of equality which is peculiar to the relations between the majority and minorities.[13]

The Court also pointed out that it would not be an easy task to define the distinction between the notions of equality in fact and equality in law, but it maintained that the notion of equality in fact "excludes the idea of a mere form of equality",[14] signifying that a mere form of equality is different from "equality in fact".

Referring to the Advisory Opinion in German Settlers in Poland (Opinion No. 6) the Court iterated that:

> "There must be equality in fact as well as ostensible legal equality in the sense of the absence of discrimination in the words of the law."[15]

The Court then provided the distinction between "equality in law" and "equality in fact" in the following passage:

[12] op. cit., at 15.

[13] op. cit., at 19.

[14] Ibid.

[15] Ibid.

> Equality in law precludes discrimination of any kind; whereas equality in fact may involve the necessity of different treatment in order to attain a result which establishes an equilibrium between different situations.[16]

The keywords in this passage are—equality in fact may involve the necessity of different treatment. The Albanian Government's act, according to the Court, failed to satisfy the requirement for "equality in fact". In their Dissenting Opinions Sir Cecil Hurst, Count Rostworowski and Judge Negulesco gave the following interpretation to the legal aspects of "equality":

> Equality in law and fact not merely excludes all discrimination between the majority and the minority but may necessitate different treatment of the majority and the minority so as to produce an equilibrium between their respective situations.[17]

The Advisory Opinion of the Permanent Court of International Justice is still valid and relevant to this day in regard to commercial/economic diplomacy. Should trade preferences between developed and developing countries be based on identical terms? This issue has been elaborated with reference to the Most-Favoured Nation Standard.

<u>The Scenario</u>

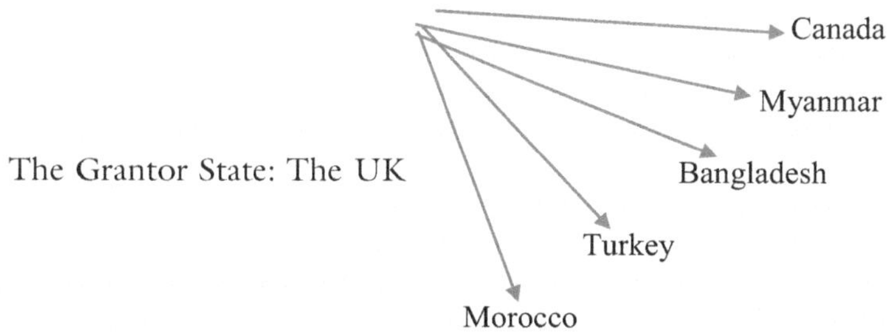

Assume that Canada approached the UK for preferential trading arrangement between themselves; but in order to avoid any discriminatory treatment the Government of the United Kingdom decided to offer same preferential treatment to every State party to the treaty based on an

[16] Ibid.

[17] op. cit., at 26.

MFN clause in it. The treaty between Canada and the UK would now be a multilateral treaty. Take, for example, that in order to maintain "equality in law" the Government of the UK allows 50% tariff reduction to all the parties to the treaty based on its MFN clause. In this example, the poorest economies, namely Bangladesh and Myanmar should deserve a higher tariff reduction.

Here is an issue which deserves the attention of the diplomatic world, particularly the diplomatic world in the developing countries. The equality in fact concept, if applied judiciously, developing countries will benefit. However, it should be borne in mind that lowering of tariffs by grantor States alone may not strengthen the trading position of a country transnationally; what is needed is "capacity building" coupled with "market access". Both these concepts have received attention in the subsequent sections of this chapter.

In writing on the negotiating techniques to be adopted by diplomats, this author maintains that diplomats should not proceed with any unachievable target (at least within the foreseeable future) of achieving globalisation of trade, as it may not happen until all the countries in the world, rich or poor alike, are able to effectively participate in the globalisation process; that is, with an appropriate capacity in terms of training culminating in the manufacturing ability to manufacture high quality products which would be marketable in the rich world.

By the same token, trade liberalisation, which is a fundamental need for allowing developing and developed States to participate at least on equal terms and gain the benefits of it. It is mutual trade that mainly develops mutual friendship—an important element of foreign policy-making for trading partners.

Ricardo's Theory of Comparative Advantage provides a fundamental idea that countries trade by virtue of being different in terms of capacity to produce or manufacture products, as the case may be, and diplomats are required to fight inequalities, and ensure that they are eventually able to compete with the States which are more capable in terms of competitiveness, capacity building, etc.

There is hardly any point in going into the details of WTO's activities, as in practical terms, they are still in the making. There exist two distinct groups of countries who are Members of the WTO. In regard to almost every single trade-related issue both sets of countries' effective participation would be essential. This is where the skills of diplomats in economic diplomacy become extremely relevant and useful. Instead of going into the details of the organisational structure of the WTO and its dispute settlement procedure, it would be more useful for diplomats to be acquainted with the following issues in particular and prepare themselves for an effective negotiation on each of the issues which have been identified later on. What is needed is a strong lobby for developing countries at the WTO platform. Diplomats are reminded of the fact that there does not exist any definitions of "developed" and "developing" countries; indeed, some of the so-called "developing" countries are now richer than some of the so-called "developed" countries. Thus, the WTO platform for trade negotiations by the rich developing countries are not entirely meaningless; they have a duty too; in addition to protecting their own trading position in the world, they should also protect the trading position of the developing world as a whole. This is not a question of a tit-for-tat situation, but on trade and investment issues, two categories of countries should be as close as possible; otherwise, the differences between these two major divisions of the countries will have an adverse effect on societies.[18] Thus, this international forum is not only a trade and investment forum, but also a societal development forum too as the position of a country as a strong trading and investment partner, makes the country concerned rich too.

The following are the particular issues on which an effective economic diplomacy is urgently needed:

1. the trade liberalisation process including the usefulness of the MFN (Most-Favoured-nation) treatment;
2. the primary purposes of WTO rules, and in what way(s) they should be different from the GATT rules;
3. the comparative advantages and disadvantages between multilateralism and bilateralism in trade;
4. trade and the protection of the environment;
5. should there be import and export restrictions in trade[19] and

[18] See further S Lester, B Mercurio, and A Davies, *World Trade Law: Text, Materials and Commentary*, Oxford, Hart Publishing, latest edition.

[19] For the footnotes 1–5, please see an extremely informative published work entitled *From GATT to the WTO: The Multilateral Trading System in the New Millennium*, published by WTO—Kluwer Law International, The Hague (2000); it contains a very

6. whether the current admission criteria for developing countries are fair.[20]

As to the dispute settlement procedures of WTO, unless they settle their disputes, by negotiations, it is really an issue with which the lawyers would be involved.[21]

10.4 Conclusions

As a concluding remark, it may be pointed out that with very enlarged consumer markets worldwide, diplomats engaged in economic/commercial diplomacy should ensure that the terms of trade are "fair" to both, developed and developing countries, and critically consider the viability of MFN system which offers a pseudo-platform for equality in transnational or cross-border trade.

good bibliography too. See also John H Jackson, *The World Trade Organisation: Constitution and Jurisprudence*, London, The Royal Institute of International Affairs (latest edition).

[20] See further P Van Den Bossche, et al., *The Law and Policy of the World Trade Organization*, Cambridge, Cambridge University Press, latest edition.

[21] Some of the good published works on WTO dispute settlement procedures are: World Trade Organization, *A Handbook on the WTO Dispute Settlement System*, Cambridge, Cambridge University Press (2011); A D Mitchell, *Legal Principles in WTO Disputes*, Cambridge, Cambridge University Press (2011).

CHAPTER 11

Economic Diplomacy at International Fora

11.1 Introduction

Article III of the Agreement Establishing the World Trade Organization states, inter alia, that:

> The WTO shall provide the forum for negotiations among its Members concerning their multinational trade relations in matters dealt with under the agreements in the Annexes to this Agreement. The WTO may also provide a forum for further negotiations among its Members concerning their multi-lateral trade solutions, and a framework for the implementation of the results of such negotiations, as may be decided by the Ministerial Conference.

The above position does clearly indicate that the diplomats engaged in economic diplomacy require skills and knowledge in negotiating terms and conditions relating to trade issues in order to protect their national interests. But what is "skill"? According to the Oxford Dictionary of English, "skill" means "the ability to do something well; expertise".[1] "Knowledge" on the other hand, stands for "information and skills acquired through experience or education, the theoretical or practical understanding of a subject".[2] An analysis of the definitions of these two

[1] Oxford, Oxford University Press (2010) at 1671.

[2] op. cit., at 976.

C. Chatterjee, *Economic Diplomacy and Foreign Policy-making*,
https://doi.org/10.1007/978-3-030-49047-8_11

terms will simply confirm the kind of expertise diplomats should possess in effecting any successful negotiation.

It is worth noticing that after the initiative taken by the developing world during the 1970s, culminating in the Resolution on the Charter of Economic Rights and Duties of States, 1974, they seem to have lost their steam. If developing countries, in general, remain aid-ridden and with huge debt burden, then of course, the question of exerting their bargaining power against their opponents would not arise; and unfortunately, that is the reality.

Together with this issue, developing countries are required to develop confidence in the minds of private foreign investors and foreign traders by changing/updating their judicial systems, where necessary, along with other incidental issues such as democratisation of their governance systems. However, the creativity in a diplomat becomes an essential requisite for carrying out a rewarding diplomacy. A diplomat would be endowed with creativity if he/she is very familiar with the contemporary commercial policies of the rich and poor countries, the important instruments that provide binding or framework principles and regulations and the gaps in those instruments.

National interest must always be protected in international economic diplomacy; but on the other hand, it is for national diplomats also to promote international policies and principles concerning international trade and investment whereby the interests of both developed and developing countries are protected. Member States of the international community should provide a system or platform at which diplomats may receive training for international diplomacy and for learning negotiating techniques and knowledge in issue of trade and investment and related disciplines. The selection process of diplomats should also receive attention of States; alternatively, the national academies of diplomacy may like to review their position in order to cope with the demands of the day.

11.2 Economic Diplomacy at an International Level

Economic diplomacy at an international level is usually concerned with two primary issues: (a) protection of the national interest when an international Convention or international Declaration or a UN Resolution may be adopted; and (b) to promote principles and standards of international economic issues including matters related to private foreign investments; that is, investments made by transnational corporations. Of course, many would also include economic diplomacy at both regional levels as well as at an international level.

It is to be emphasised however that economic diplomacy at an international level should not be allowed to be dominated by any particular country or a group of countries—the notion of false bargaining power should be changed. What is needed is the identification of issues and an articulate submission of those issues emphasising the national interest and the need for developing new principles and standards of international business including private foreign investment.

Economic diplomacy has both a narrow and a broader aspect—whereas the narrow aspect of it is concerned with the protection of the national interest, the development of principles and norms about inter-State and international commerce relates to the broader aspect of economic diplomacy. Economic diplomacy at an international level may not disregard the issue of the protection of the legitimate national interest when such interests have been clearly identified and articulated. This brings the issue of the expertise in diplomats in preparing their arguments before international conferences or even for inter-State economic diplomacy. Selection of diplomats for presenting their cases on behalf of their States should be carefully made; it is not necessarily the most educationally qualified individual who might perform this function competently and effectively—his or her knowledge based on practical experience in that subject matter of diplomacy coupled with his/her thorough understanding of the issues not only to protect the sending State's national interest but also those others whose national interests are also to be protected would be essential. This point has been further developed in a separate section of this chapter.

Economic diplomacy in its wider aspect should be addressed to the issue in which the international community has common interests or should have such interests and the means of protecting those interests. The Rio Declaration of 1992 is an instrument which identified, inter alia, many of the common interests or which should be regarded as the common interest of the international community in relation to the protection of the environment. Article 30 of the Charter of Economic Rights and Duties of State, 1974 rightly identified the common responsibilities of the international community in regard to the protection of the environment. Article 30 of the Charter provides that:

> The protection, preservation and enhancement of the environment for the present and future generations is the responsibility of all States. All States shall endeavour to establish their own environmental and developmental policies in conformity with such responsibility. The environmental policies of all States should enhance and not adversely affect the present and future development potential of developing countries. All States have the responsibility to ensure that activities within their jurisdiction or control do not cause damage to the environment of other States or of areas beyond the limits of national jurisdiction. All States should co-operate in evolving international norms and regulations in the field of the environment.

Article 29 of the Charter provides, inter alia, that:

> The sea-bed and ocean floor and the subsoil thereof, beyond the limits of national jurisdiction, as well as the resources of the area, are the common heritage of mankind ... all States shall ensure that the exploration of the area and exploitation of its resources are carried out exclusively for peaceful purposes and that the benefits derived therefrom are shared equitably by all States, taking into account the particular interests and needs of developing countries...

This aspect of international economic diplomacy is extremely important; and it can be strengthened if international economic diplomacy accords sufficient importance to it.

11.3 Preparation for Economic Diplomacy at an International Level

The importance of preparation for economic diplomacy at an international level may not be over-emphasised. The term "preparation" means something done to get ready for an event or undertaking. This has to be done in accordance with the core objectives of the event which may not be done without a proper understanding of the event.

It is to be pointed out that in preparing oneself, one must bear in mind two important issues among others: (a) he/she has to protect his/her national interest in respect of the subject/matter/theme for which he/she would be confronting others; and (b) that the other delegates would also make attempts to do so. Thus, it is important to realise that others' points of view in relation to their national interest have to be considered before any resolution or decision reached. A diplomat should possess a thorough understanding of the issues including their historical bases and gradual development, if any.

The contemporary development in the commercial world pertaining to the topic must also be borne in mind, and where necessary, relate it to the topic included in the agenda. Where an issue is multifaceted, each of its facets, namely political, socio-economic and even legal dimensions must be clearly identified and analysed. It is therefore important that national diplomats are fully aware of the recent developments in relation to the topic(s) which may be discussed at a regional and a truly international level.

Economic diplomacy is at the root of all other forms of diplomacy—thus, it should be dealt with care, sensitivity and tact. It would be unwise for any national diplomat to jeopardise the sending State's commercial relationship with a receiving State, particularly when the latter is commercially stronger than the former. "Commercial" in this context should be treated as a generic term encompassing trade, commerce, investment, services and related issues. The so-called bi-lateral foreign policy between two countries is often shaped by the mutual commercial interests of the two parties, unless the lesser party has decided to follow what may be described as diplomacy of dependency. Through appropriate policy-making, the lesser States should be able to strengthen their commercial position by indigenous means in conjunction with the advice of experts.

Preparation for economic diplomacy therefore primarily entails the following: historical development of the issue or problem; attitudes of the actors in the mainstream commercial world towards that issue or problem; the issue of the protection of the national interest; the issue of the protection of the interest of the international community pertaining to the issue or problem and the issue of the protection of the interests of the disadvantaged States, if the issue or problem is a matter of international concern.

11.4 How Economic Diplomacy at an International Level Fails

There may be a variety of reasons for the failure of economic diplomacy at an international level: (a) a rigid view maintained by Sovereign States as to their sovereignty including their national interests; (b) the lack of understanding on the part of the participants of the theme of economic diplomacy; (c) the lack of preparation on the part of participants for a formidable negotiating position and (d) the lack of determination to implement accord which may have been reached at a negotiation stage. Like, for example, the Rio Declaration of 1992, which presented a sound initiative by the developing countries, simply did not materialise in the proper sense of the term primarily for three reasons: (a) there exists a rather strange perception in the minds of sovereign States that "Declarations" have no legally binding status, without any justification for that perception; (b) that in drafting the provisions, the developing States failed to appreciate that it would be difficult for the developed States, which have traditionally been the home of private foreign investors (often described as transnational or multinational corporations) to accept what may be described as "the polluter pays principle" (Principle 13 of the Declaration) overnight; it should have been phasal. On the other side of the coin, the question remains, how many of the developing States have been taking positive action for ensuring that the pollution process of the environment must be decreased? In this connection, it would be interesting to note that since the conclusion of the Rio Declaration, hardly any bi-lateral investment treaty seems to have incorporated Rio's provisions, in particular, Principle 13 of it. In other words, in negotiating or prescribing any guidelines at an international level, the representatives or diplomats of State should take a realistic view of the world. It has to be admitted however that in principle, the protection of the environment is an issue which needs an urgent attention of the world community, but a realistic time-frame to achieve it would be the most prudent move on it and (c) in developing guidelines at an international level, the representatives of or participants from every State should bear in mind the issue of the national interests of the other States which are jealously guarded by each participant and yet, certain common denominators will have to be found in the interest of the international community. This issue in fact hinges upon the strategies of negotiations—in order for developing countries to achieve their objectives, they are required to appreciate the aspirations of the developed States; as otherwise, the twin shall never meet.

In a negotiation process, there is no room for emotion; diplomats and representatives of developing States must prepare their strategies by referring to the strategies that their colleagues belonging to the developed States might rely upon. The idea is not to create a climate of confrontation, but to develop a friendly atmosphere by appreciating each other's demands. The UN Convention on the Law of the Sea, 1982 (UNCLOS

III) is a good example to refer to in which position all kinds of States have been attempted to protect in regard to the sea resources.

11.5 The Role of Developing Countries in Strengthening Economic Diplomacy

There exists a perception that developing countries, in general, have a rather insignificant role to play in developing and strengthening of international economic diplomacy; this is an unsustainable perception, but it has damaged the position of developing countries in strengthening international economic diplomacy. The crux of diplomacy, economic or otherwise, is negotiation for a deal which would be profitable and beneficial for both the parties concerned. If negotiation is not allowed, then there is no diplomacy; it would be an act of domination of one party over the other.

Principles and standards if established by domination will be subject to breach. One should reflect on the reasons for initiating an agenda for a New International Economic Order in 1974, in which initiative was taken by the developing countries to register their protests against the old international economic order which was a product of the Bretton Woods arrangement at which time the current developing countries' voices did not exist. In other words, international economic diplomacy must be based on the basis of non-discrimination, fairness and in the interest of the international community as a whole. In developing principles and standards of international economic diplomacy, special attention must be paid to the issue of the protection of the interest of the least developed, land-locked and other countries which are in a special position, whether for geographic reasons or otherwise.

As stated before, "bargaining power" in diplomacy is often incorrectly used, and indeed abused. It stands for the power to negotiate,[3] which is nothing but an exercise to reach a decision by sustainable arguments put forward by both or all parties to the process. Developing countries' contribution to international economic and commercial diplomacy should not be disregarded—take for example, the UN Resolution on

[3] See further C Chatterjee, *International Law and Diplomacy*, London, Routledge (2010) at 81.

Permanent Sovereignty over Natural Resources, 1962,[4] which has formed part of customary rules of international law, or their idea to create the concept of the Exclusive Economic Zone which has found a place in the UN Convention on the Law of the Sea (UNCLOS III) or the Stockholm Declaration on the Protection of the Environment 1972 or the Rio Declaration of 1992 on the same theme. The Charter of Economic Rights and Duties of States 1974,[5] although failed to be adopted by the contemporary international community, it still provides some of the fundamental principles and policies which should form the basis for a balanced international economic diplomacy.

The days of polarised economic diplomacy are numbered. Some of the developing countries are now major players in the business world; take for example, Brazil, China and India; Indonesia is a resourceful country and should soon be a significant player on the markets. On the other hand, one of the fundamental policies of international economic diplomacy would be to ensure that developing countries would eventually be recognisable participants in international economic diplomacy and in the commercial world. Furthermore, the developing countries' economic and commercial strengths are to be improved by proactive international co-operation, as the developed countries may not stay developed, because they need larger markets for their products. Hence the need for a dynamic economic diplomacy to keep pace with the demands of a fast-changing world.

11.6 Conclusions

There are a significant number of issues relating to trade and investment, intellectual property, accession of new applicant members, tariff issue including most-favoured nation treatment to name but a few with which diplomats representing their States should be extremely familiar with a view to strengthening their position within the WTO by negotiating favourable terms in regard to the issues identified above. Only a brief account of a limited number of issues are discussed now.

[4] Resolution No. 1803 of 1962.

[5] UN Resolution No. 3261.

a. Non-discrimination including the MFN treatment

The popular definition has been that an absence of discrimination amounts to non-discrimination, but for lawyers two fundamental elements deserve attention: (a) an intent to discriminate; and (b) the effect of discrimination (otherwise known as "disparate impact").[6] These essentials are now briefly discussed.

b. Intent

Although "intent" of the wrongdoer attracts the attention of the criminal lawyers, the use of "intent" as a factor in GATT non-discrimination has provoked controversy, in fact, WTO Panels and the WTO Appellate Body questioned the appropriateness of looking into "intent". From an academic perspective, it may be pointed out that the term "intent" has two aspects: (a) subjective; and (b) objective. Whereas subjective intent refers to the motive of legislators or regulators in putting the measure into effect, objective intent represents the "overall" intent of the government in adopting the measure.[7] Leaving all academic views aside, from a diplomatic perspective, for the purpose of policy-making, what a diplomat should look into is whether discrimination of any kind caused by the imposition of tariffs or by virtue of a particular type of classification of products would have a disproportionate impact on foreign goods as compared to domestic goods. Given the fact not sufficient emphasis is placed on "intent", it may be maintained that the "effect" of discrimination is a means of confirming discrimination. But it is de facto as opposed to de jure discrimination that no remedies may be made available to the injured party. That the current practice of applying the most-favoured nation standard does not really create "equality" among trading partners has already received attention in Chapter 10 of this work.

c. Then, of course, there is the issue of the Generalised System of Preferences (GSP) under which scheme whereas developed countries are not supposed to impose any import duty on the products entering into developed countries, but products from developed countries in entering into GSP-led countries would be required to pay import

[6] See further S Lester, B Mercurio, and A Davies, World Trade Law: Text, Materials and Commentary, op. cit., at 261.

[7] See further Lester, Mercurio and Davies, op. cit., at 262.

duties, but which system is subject to a variety of exceptions; see, for example, the US GSP System.[8] This issue also needs the urgent attention of the developing States.

d. Finally, the issue of accession conditions for developing States to the WTO. Assume that an applicant State's application for accession has otherwise been found suitable, the answers to the questions they are required to provide are quite difficult for them. They are required to successfully satisfy the following stages:

Stage 1

"Tell us about yourself"—the question remains what may a developing State seeking its membership tell the WTO authorities? Its export and investment records are usually poor; so is her infrastructure. An Applicant State is required to import on all aspects of its trade and economic policies in order to convince the WTO that it would be able to fulfil its obligations under the WTO agreements, and also to submit a memorandum on their policies which will be examined by a WTO Working Party established for the purpose.

Stage 2

In the event of the Working Party making satisfactory progress with the examination of the Applicant State's trade and economic policies, the second stage of the process will be initiated. This stage entails an even more difficult question—what can you offer to the WTO as an individual Member? At this stage, bi-lateral negotiations on market access start between the Applicant for membership and individual Members. The new Member's market access commitments and concessions must eventually apply equally to all WTO Members owing to the MFN treatment obligation.[9] According to Van Den Bossche, these bi-lateral negotiations can be very difficult.[10]

[8] See further S K Chatterjee, "Forty Years of International Action for Trade Liberalisation" 23 *Journal of World Trade* (Geneva) (1989).

[9] See further P Van Den Bossche, *The Law and Policy of the World Trade Organisation*, op. cit., Chapter 2.

[10] op. cit.

Stage 3

This stage entails drafting of the membership terms. The Working Party finalises the terms of accession, the Protocol of accession and schedules of the market access commitments, in addition to the concessions allowed to the Applicant. This document is submitted to the Ministerial Conference or the General Council.

Stage 4

This stage is also known as the "decision" stage; decisions are taken by the Ministerial Conference or the General Council by consensus; and in the event of not achieving a consensus by either of the above-named institutions, by a two-thirds majority of the WTO members; if an affirmative decision is reached in favour of the Applicant, it accedes to the WTO thirty days after it has deposited its instrument of ratification of the membership treaty, otherwise known as the Protocol of Accession.[11]

The WTO accession procedures clearly leave room for hard diplomatic negotiations with skills and knowledge, and these negotiations must pay attention to the obligations each country would be able to satisfy. On the other hand, if any developing State is not a member of the WTO, her trade with the other Members of the organisation may be adversely affected.

This is not the place to discuss the fairness or unfairness of the trade terms in the contemporary business world; the purpose of this Chapter is to draw the attention of diplomats that unless they are able to present their united views in an articulate and logical fashion, they might not succeed in their efforts to change anything which would go in their favour.

[11] See further P Van Den Bossche, op. cit., Chapter 2

CHAPTER 12

Economic Diplomacy and Private Foreign Investment

12.1 Introduction

Economic diplomacy is a term which should not receive any narrow interpretation; it encompasses, inter alia, trade, banking, finance, investment and even negotiating techniques in concluding economic agreements with other States. Private foreign investments in host countries which are based on bi-lateral investment treaties (which may take different titles) are a product of economic diplomacy between the parties to such treaties. These treaties which are governed by the principles of public international law create binding obligations for the parties concerned. They also represent many aspects of state practice in regard to private foreign investment. It is however possible for the parties to a treaty to incorporate additional clauses agreed to between themselves.

Private foreign investments usually take place between three sets of countries: (a) developed and developed; (b) developed and developing and (c) advanced developing and developing. It is the purpose of this chapter to examine how economic policies of the parties to a treaty become evident in such treaties. Attention has also been paid to State contracts which are the usual type of contracts signed by governments of developing countries with private foreign investors (usually transnational corporations) and their impact on investment projects, and how economic diplomacy should be applied in order to create confidence in the minds of private foreign investors.

C. Chatterjee, *Economic Diplomacy and Foreign Policy-making*,
https://doi.org/10.1007/978-3-030-49047-8_12

12.2 Economic Diplomacy and Risks in Private Foreign Investments

When private foreign investments are made under State contracts the sovereignty-based risks may not be avoided, but the other usual risks perceived by the public, in general, namely transfer risks, currency risks, etc. may be avoided by contractual arrangements made between the public entity and the private foreign investor. Sovereignty-based risks in this context would mean, for example, nationalisation in the public interest or change of legislation (legislation risks), etc. The nationalisation risk is almost non-existent now[1]; it was a risk during the decolonisation period. The real risks in developing countries, in general, however are: (a) environmental; and (b) judicial. Whereas environmental damages may have far-reaching adverse effect in the future, unless the private foreign investor is made subject to Article 13 (polluter pays principle) under the Rio Declaration of 1992. Article 13 of that Declaration provides that:

> States shall develop national law regarding liability and compensation for the victims of pollution and other environmental damage. States shall also co-operate in an expeditious and more determined manner to develop further international law regarding liability and compensation for adverse effect of environmental damage caused by activities within their jurisdiction or control to areas beyond their jurisdiction.

Judicial risk, on the other hand, has a deterrent effect on private foreign investors. It is important for host countries to create confidence in the minds of private foreign investors in judiciaries of host countries whereby disputes arising out of private foreign investment agreements are promptly settled by the local courts in an unbiased fashion and effectively enforced against judgement debtors. The lack of confidence in the judiciary has a direct bearing upon the choice of jurisdiction and the choice of the governing law of the foreign investment contract. Instead of choosing the jurisdiction (the courts) and the governing law of the host country, which is the place of performance, private foreign investment-related disputes are, in general, governed by the law of the investor's country and the courts in that jurisdiction assume jurisdiction, unless, of course, disputes

[1] See further C Chatterjee, "The Reality of Risks in Private Foreign Investments", *International Company and Commercial Law Review* (1996).

are referred to the International Centre for Settlement of Investment Disputes (ICSID) or other arbitration procedures.

Here, in the context of judicial risk, Economic diplomacy cannot succeed unless the developing host States improve their judicial systems—this is not to suggest that the judiciaries of all developing countries are unreliable or incompetent, but, on the other hand, the fact remains that these judiciaries can be slow in rendering judgements in relation to private foreign investment contracts. Private foreign investors do not even wish to exhaust local remedies which are, in fact, an insult to the developing host States. Unless any radical reform is achieved by the developing States, in general, in this regard, economic diplomacy in their attempts to change the minds of private foreign investors must fail. This issue has also received attention in discussing the common features of bi-lateral investment treaties in this chapter.

In an effort to encourage private foreign investors to invest in developing host States, economic diplomacy should address the following issues in particular: (a) to minimise risks by not resorting to illegal nationalisation or taking of foreign assets located in a host State; (b) to apply non-discriminatory treatment to all private foreign investors engaged in the same sector of the economy in a host country; (c) to provide protection to private foreign investors to the best of their ability[2] and (d) to develop confidence in the minds of these investors as to the competence of their judiciaries and judicial systems and the promptness in settling any dispute arising under each private foreign investment agreement. Many of the developed countries, on the other hand, do not, in general, suffer any of the deficiencies stated above.

12.3 Economic Diplomacy for Encouragement of Private Foreign Investment

Economic diplomacy has a significant role to play to encourage private foreign investments in a host State. There are certain prerequisites however which should be considered prior to inviting a private foreign investor into the country: (a) the choice of the industry; (b) availability of human resources from the country; (c) availability of most of the

[2] See *Asian Agricultural Products Ltd v Sri Lanka*, 30 *International Legal Materials* (1991) 577.

materials required for it; (d) the linkage with the other sectors of the economy and (e) the nature of economic relationship with the country to which the private foreign investor belongs. These prerequisites should be considered by the country herself rather than relying upon any external agency, as which industry would be the most appropriate for the country from her socio-economic point of view may be best considered by the country herself.

On the other hand, in order to convince a private foreign investor to invest in a country, it must be satisfied with the following:

a. That the country observes the principle of State responsibility of public international law. Under this principle, a host country is required to provide protection to private foreign investors. "Protection" in this context would mean protection of the investment from illegal nationalisation or taking of the foreign assets. An act of nationalisation would be illegal, for example, when it is carried out indiscriminately and not in the public interest. Whether the grounds of the public interest in a particular case is justifiable or not is not to be considered by an application of legal rules only. Sovereign authorities have this prerogative in this matter,[3] but it is expected that they will exercise this power in genuine circumstances. See *Luther v Sagor*.

   Among other cases on this point of the taking of foreign assets in the public interest, two cases may be referred to. In 1972, Libya illegally took the assets of BP (The British Petroleum Company), Texaco (a US Petroleum Corporation) and Calasiatic (another US Petroleum Corporation) without invoking the grounds of the public interest; in fact, the Libyan authorities' act in this regard was also discriminatory because it did not nationalise the assets of a French company engaged in that sector of investment. This also evidenced the fact that Libya did not have a coherent policy to nationalise the petroleum sector of her economy.[4] Of course, the Libyan act strained its diplomatic relations with the governments of the United Kingdom and the United States which led to the severance of diplomatic relations with those countries. This adversely affected the

[3] Luther v Sagor (1921) 1 KB 456.

[4] For a full discussion of those cases, see 53 *International Law Reports*, 227 and 589.

economic relationship between Libya and the United Kingdom and the United States for a considerable period of time.

On the other hand, nationalisation or an act of taking of foreign assets may be deemed legal when a government does so on the grounds of the genuine public interest, as was done by the tribunal in the Government of the State of Kuwait and the American Independent Oil Company (AMINOIL).[5] In 1948, the Ruler of Kuwait granted a Concession to the American Independent Oil Company (AMINOIL), a US company incorporated into the State of Delaware, for exploration and exploitation of petroleum and natural gas in what was then called the Kuwait "Neutral Zone". Kuwait attained her independence in 1961, and in 1962, its constitution was promulgated. By a treaty of July 1965 between Kuwait and Saudi Arabia, the neutral zone was renamed as the "Divided Zone", which was to be shared between these two countries. AMINOIL's Concession was situated in the Kuwait part of the Divided Zone.

There followed a series of events which adversely affected AMINOIL's position in Kuwait. The Concession contained a stabilisation clause, but the financial clauses were modified by a Supplementary Agreement of 1961 with a view to, inter alia, increasing payments to the Ruler, and subjecting the foreign company to the local income tax law. Based on the Tehran Agreement of 1971 concluded between the Gulf States and a number of major oil companies and various resolutions passed by the Organisation of Petroleum Exporting Countries (OPEC), the posted price of oil was increased.

In 1971, the Government acquired 60 per cent interest in AMINOIL, and in 1975, the Government took over the entire Concession of the Kuwait Oil Company leaving AMINOIL as the sole private company engaged in the petroleum sector in Kuwait. In the same year, the Abu Dhabi formula was formally enforced against it with the end in view that the Government would be gifted with more favourable terms of business in the petroleum sector. In September 1977, by its Decree Law No 124, the Government of Kuwait terminated the Agreement with AMINOIL in the national

[5] The text of the Award has been reproduced in 21 *International Legal Materials* (1982) 976.

interest and the company's Concession was eventually entrusted to the Kuwait Oil Company.

AMINOIL protested against the takeover, and in December 1977, instituted arbitration proceedings against the Government pursuant to Article 18 of the Concession Agreement of 1948. In this connection, it would be appropriate to refer to the provisions which were perceived to have the effect of stabilising the investment of the foreign company.

b. Private foreign investors usually look into some other issues, namely the history of nationalisation of private foreign investments; litigation against investors or investors suing the host State; failure to pay its due to private foreign investors; failure to observe the international minimum standard towards these investors or failure to observe national treatment in favour of private foreign investors (under the standards of the national treatment, the privileges and facilities that a host country offers to its own domestic industries, the foreign enterprises engaged in the same sector of the economy must be offered the same privileges and facilities); how many foreign entities of good standing operate in that country and the Missions of foreign countries, etc.

   Information of the above nature is very useful for economic diplomacy. In order to attract private foreign investors, it is important to justify, by evidence, that the host country concerned does not present risks. In this context, negotiating techniques in contracts become an essential element of economic diplomacy.

c. State contracts may fail all economic diplomacy because a sovereign might on the grounds of the public interest abrogate any private investment agreement. What is to be considered is whether a sovereign authority represented by its government has abused its power. As explained earlier that any abuse of power by a sovereign is a matter which may not be considered by applying any principle of law. However, abuse of power by a sovereign will exclude it from the general domain of economic diplomacy. But there may be cases when a sovereign may genuinely be required to exercise its power in the public interest and in that event, it may not be accused of being in abuse of its power.

   It is through the vehicle of State contracts that most private foreign investments in developing countries are carried out. Unless the diplomatic relations between the investor's State and the host

State are strained, the incidence of the risk of nationalisation/taking of foreign assets would be minimal. In this connection one should not refer to the acts of nationalisation/taking of foreign assets which took place during the decolonisation period as those acts were inevitable during that period in order to regain ownership in and control over their (the newly independent States) natural or other resources.

Ideally, private foreign investment in a host country should be based on reciprocity; however, in the case of developing host States, reciprocity may not take place. Host governments should not encourage the entry of private foreign investors in an unrestrained fashion, as in that event, the entire economy or the most important sectors of it might be taken over by them. By the same token, host countries should consider whether the duration of private foreign investment contracts should be unduly long. These contracts should be accompanied by turn-key contracts whereby the local workforce may have an opportunity to learn the industry/project and operate it.

d. In terms of the protection of the national interest, economic diplomacy has two dimensions: (a) that the State's interest must be protected; and (b) that it must not be protected at the cost of reciprocity, where possible, with the state of the private foreign investor. As a matter of practice, bi-lateral investment treaties provide for reciprocity; however, as developing countries are not usually capable of reciprocating with the developed investors, bi-lateral investment treaties should provide for capacity building for the developing partner. An examination of the basic features of bi-lateral investment treaties has taken place in the next Section of this chapter. The purpose of inviting private foreign investors in developing host countries is also to learn from the investors.

12.4 A Critical Examination of Certain Selected Bi-Lateral Investment Treaties

Negotiation of bi-lateral investment treaties requires skills in economic diplomacy. The purpose is to ensure that the terms and conditions on which such treaties are concluded would be beneficial for the host State (the State on behalf of which the diplomat negotiates). Training of local people or capacity building should be one of the important components of such treaties. Of course, the other party to the treaty would also negotiate for the best benefits it may derive from such treaties.

In many of these treaties the two parties' position is unequal—one is a developed country and the other is a developing country. However, treaties between two countries of similar standing are also available. It would be interesting to examine the treaties which have been concluded (a) between two developed countries; (b) between a developed and a developing country and (c) between a middle-grade country (neither very developed nor developing) and a developed country.

Four points should be highlighted in this context: (a) that both developed and middle-grade countries as parties to an investment treaty would like to ensure that their profits from their investments are not subject to any foreign exchange control, that is, they must be allowed to remit their profits and incomes from the host country to their home country in a chosen hard currency; (b) that they are not discriminated against other private foreign investors engaged in the same sector of the economy; (c) that are granted certain financial relief in the form of tax concessions, etc. and (d) that assurances are provided by host countries as to the protection of their investments.

As to the remittance of their profits and incomes in a chosen hard currency, the host country's representatives should seriously consider whether such remittances outweigh the benefits they may derive from the treaty arrangements. Secondly, most of these treaties, particularly those concluded between a developed and a developing country are one-sided in that there cannot be any reciprocity between the countries—the developing host States are unable to contribute to the home country (the investor's country) in any way; unless of course, a BOT (build, operate and transfer) arrangement is built into the treaty.[6]

There also has become evident a high degree of stereotyping in negotiating drafting these treaties perhaps in the belief that the private foreign investor would not otherwise accept the treaty obligations which belief

[6] Under a BOT arrangement, the foreign investor will be required to set up an industry which would be beneficial to the host country, and which would require the foreign investor to train the local people in learning the production process such that eventually they are able to manufacture high quality products which would be sold on the investor's markets. This arrangement has at least two direct benefits: development of skills and foreign income for the host country.

should be rationalised in order to avoid "one-size fits all" policy. Each host country's requirements for development are often different. Furthermore, the treaty obligations are often unequal for the parties which have been explained in a subsequent Section of this chapter. These issues are important to bear in mind as the actual contract of investment will be based on such treaties.

12.5 An Examination of Certain Selected Bi-Lateral Investment Treaties

12.5.1 The Agreement Between the Government of the Kingdom of Denmark and the Government of the Russian Federation Concerning the Promotion and Reciprocal Protection of Investments, 1996[7]

This Treaty consists of 12 Articles:

Article 1—Definitions
Article 2—Promotion and Reciprocal Protection of Investments
Article 3—Treatment of Investments
Article 4—Expropriation
Article 5—Compensation for losses
Article 6—Transfer of payments in connection with an Investment
Article 7—Subrogation
Article 8—Disputes between an Investor of one Contracting Party and the other Contracting Party
Article 9—Disputes between the Contracting Parties
Article 10—Consultations
Article 11—Application of this Agreement
Article 12—Entry into Force, Duration and Termination of the Agreement.

The Preamble to the Treaty provides that:

[7] The text of the Agreement has been reproduced in the United Nations Treaty Series, vol. 2009, I-34468. This treaty came into force on 25 September 1996.

> Desiring to create favourable conditions for increasing investments by investors of one Contracting Party in the territory of the other Contracting Party;
> Recognising that a fair and equitable treatment of investments on a reciprocal basis will serve this aim.

The Article on Definitions (Article 1) defines certain terms such as "investment", "returns", "investor", and "territory". Under Article 2 (Promotion and Reciprocal Protection of Investments) the parties undertook the obligation to provide full protection and security in the territory of the other contracting party. It also provides that:

> Neither Contracting Party shall in any way impair by unreasonable or discriminatory measures the management, maintenance, use, enjoyment or disposal of investments in its territory of investors of the other Contracting Party.

In fact, this provision refers to the principle of State Responsibility under public international law. However, the term "full protection" has provoked controversy in the past. This issue arose before an ICSID tribunal in the AAPL arbitration.

Article 3 (Treatment of Investments) provides for what are known as "national treatment" and "most favoured nation treatment". According to this Article:

> Each Contracting Party shall accord investments made by investors of the other Contracting Party in its territory fair and equitable treatment no less favourable than that which it accords to investments of its own investors or to investments of investors of any third State, whichever treatment is favourable.

Similar provisions have also been made as regards the management, maintenance, use, enjoyment or disposal of their investments fair and equitable treatment "no less favourable than that which it accords to its own investors or to investors of any third State, whatever treatment is more favourable." Each Contracting Party protected its position as regards special preferences or privileges resulting from:

a. its participation in a free trade area, customs or economic union or similar multilateral agreement;[8]
b. the agreement in the field of economic co-operation of the Russian Federation with the States that constituted the former Union of Soviet Socialist Republic.

Article 4 (Expropriation) is an inevitable provision in such treaties of private foreign investments—that is, investments that are protected from nationalisation, expropriation or any other form of taking by the host State except for

> ... measures taken in the public interest on a basis of non-discrimination and against prompt, adequate and effective compensation. Such compensation shall amount to the value of the investment expropriated immediately before the expropriation or impending expropriation became public knowledge.

Compensation is usually paid in a freely transferable currency and includes interest at the normal economic rate "established on a market basis from the date of expropriation until the date of payment." Incidentally, tribunals, as a matter of practice, award "appropriate" compensation rather than "adequate" compensation as prescribed by the Hull formula. Interestingly enough, developed countries still provide for "adequate" compensation contrary to the provision for "appropriate" compensation prescribed by the UN General Assembly Resolution entitled Permanent Sovereignty over Natural Resources, 1962[9] which has formed part of customary international law. Paragraph (2) of Article 4 deserves some comments. This paragraph provides that:

> The investor affected shall have the right, under the law of the Contracting Party making the expropriation, to prompt review, by a judicial or other independent authority of that Contracting Party, of his or its case and of the valuation of his or its investment in accordance with the principles set out in this Article.

[8] This provision related to Denmark.

[9] Resolution No. 1803.

Article 5 (Compensation for Losses)—if an investor suffers losses in the host country owing to war, other armed conflicts, a state of national emergency or other similar circumstances shall be indemnified in a manner which is no less favourable than that which it accords to its own investors or to investors of any third State. Payments shall be made without delay and be freely transferable currency.

Article 6 (Transfer of payments in connection with an Investment) is concerned with transfer of payments in connection with an investment.

Article 7 (Subrogation)—this Article provides that:

> where one Contracting Party or its designated agency has granted any guarantee against non-Economic risks to its investor with regard to his investment in the territory if the other Contracting Party, the latter shall recognise the right of the first Contracting Party or its designated agency by virtue of subrogation to the rights of the investor when payment has been made under the guarantee of the first Contracting Party or its designated agency.

Article 8 (Disputes between an Investor of one Contracting Party and the other Contracting Party)—according to this Article, in the event of a dispute arising between the investor of one Contracting Party and the other Contracting Party in connection with an investment on the territory of the other Contracting Party shall be attempted to be sorted by negotiations between the parties in dispute, and if this should fail, then the dispute shall be referred to arbitration for settlement.

Article 9 (Disputes between the Contracting Parties)—the provisions of this Article too provides for settlement of disputes initially by negotiations between the parties concerned, and if these attempts fail, then it will be referred to an arbitral tribunal.

Article 10 (Consultations)—this procedure will be adopted for the purposes of reviewing the implementation or application of the Agreement. Consultation shall be held on the proposal of one of the Contracting Parties.

Whereas Article 11 (Application of this Agreement) is concerned with the territorial application of the Agreement, the subject matter of Article 12 (Entry into Force, Duration and Termination of the Agreement) is concerned with the procedures for bringing the Agreement into force; its duration and the procedure for terminating it.

12.5.2 *Agreement Between the Government of Mongolia and the Government of the Kingdom of Denmark Concerning the Promotion and Reciprocal Protection of Investments*[10]

The objectives of this Agreement are very similar to those in the Agreement between Denmark and Russia discussed above. This Agreement consists of 16 Articles.

Article 1—Definitions
Article 2—Promotion and Protection of Investments
Article 3—Treatment of Investments
Article 4—Exceptions
Article 5—Expropriation and Compensation
Article 6—Compensation for Losses
Article 7—Transfer of Capital and Returns
Article 8—Subrogation
Article 9—Disputes between a Contracting Party and an Investor
Article 10—Disputes between the Contracting Parties
Article 11—Consultations
Article 12—Applicability of this Agreement
Article 13—Amendments
Article 14—Territorial Extension
Article 15—Entry into Force
Article 16—Duration and Termination.

The differences between these two Agreements are minimal. "Exceptions" under Article 4 relate to national treatment, and membership of a party to any existing or future regional economic integration or customs union.

[10]The text of this Agreement has been reproduced in the UN Treaty Series. This Treaty came into force on 2 March 1996.

12.5.3 *Agreement Between the Government of the Republic of Korea and the Government of the Republic of the Philippines for the Promotion and Protection of Investments, 1994*[11]

This Agreement also shares similarities with the two other Agreements referred to above other than that it incorporated a separate Article entitled "Promotion of Joint Venture" (Article 7) which provides that:

1. The Contracting Parties shall encourage and promote joint ventures between the two States in all possible fields subject to relevant laws and regulations.
2. The Contracting Parties shall also encourage and facilitate export trade of the products from such joint ventures to the third State and to their own States in accordance with the laws and regulations of the two States.

This is a good provision; indeed, this should be one of the important purposes for concluding reciprocal arrangements—between Contracting Parties to bi-lateral investment agreements. The mutual benefits that the parties will derive from such an arrangement are obvious.

12.5.4 *Agreement Between the Government of the United Kingdom of Great Britain and Northern Ireland and the Government of the Oriental Republic of Uruguay for the Promotion and Protection of Investments, 1991*[12]

The provisions of this Agreement are very similar to those which have been referred to above. It consists of 13 Articles.

Article 1—Definitions
Article 2—Promotion and Protection of Investment
Article 3—Treatment of Investments
Article 4—Compensation for Losses
Article 5—Expropriation
Article 6—Repatriation of Investment and Returns

[11] The text of this Agreement has been reproduced in the UN Treaty Series, Vol. 2032, I 35081.

[12] The text of this Agreement has been reproduced in the UN Treaty Series, Vol. 2004, I 34348; this Agreement came into force on 1 August, 1997.

Article 7—Exceptions
Article 8—Settlement of Disputes between a National or Company and a Host State
Article 9—Disputes between the Contracting Parties
Article 10—Subrogation
Article 11—Territorial Extension
Article 12—Entry into Force
Article 13—Duration and Termination.

These bi-lateral investment treaties were selected to evidence the fact that irrespective of the economic standing of the Contracting Parties, each of them incorporates similar provisions rather than incorporating provisions which would suit the needs particularly of the Contracting Parties. Investment contracts based on such treaties do, in general, contain provisions, which in many ways share similarities. What is to be considered is whether the range of benefits, including capacity building, may be derived from the investment arrangements made with private foreign investors.

12.6 Comments

Bi-lateral Investment Treaties (BITs) are, in general, particular about protecting the interests of private foreign investors, and to that effect include protective clauses. In fact, they include some of the established principles and standards of public international law. Nevertheless, these treaties represent a degree of what may be described as "stereotyped" diplomacy. Furthermore, the balance of obligations tilt towards host States in that they are required to protect the interests of private foreign investors almost in all respects, but in return, the obligations of these investors towards host countries are of a limited nature.

There is no harm in incorporating clauses in these treaties whereby the interests of host countries will also be promoted in a meaningful way. In most cases, where the Contracting Parties are of different economic standing, the issue of reciprocity becomes meaningless. It is through such treaties that the economic strength of developing countries should be achieved, and diplomacy in negotiating such treaties should be directed at that objective; otherwise, it defeats the whole purpose of concluding such treaties.

In concluding bi-lateral investment treaties, the issue of cost-effectiveness for host countries should be seriously considered. One of the principal purposes of concluding such treaties is to attain economic self-sufficiency and to increase its capacity to access export markets. The other objective of such treaties must be to protect and promote the interests of both the parties—the private foreign investor and the host State.

12.7 Conclusions

Economic diplomacy at a bi-lateral level is about achieving the best through negotiation with the other party. The traditional perception that diplomacy is based on bargaining power is rather misleading; it is the negotiating skills of the stronger of the parties that currently matter most. Economic diplomacy should aim at developing interdependence between the States concerned, which forms friendship and leads to peaceful relations between them.

Economic diplomacy may be used in any sphere of business; including exchange of knowledge and skills. In fact, instead of negotiating for high technology, or high-technology-based projects, economic diplomacy should be directed at seeking knowledge and skills from those who are able to transfer them.

It has already been explained that a special kind of knowledge and expertise would be necessary for conducting economic diplomacy successfully. In so far as private foreign investment agreements are concerned, the purpose is not only to develop sectors of an economy in a developing country with the help of private foreign investors but also to develop indigenous technology and industries in addition to knowledge and skills. Trade and investment create friendship.

CHAPTER 13

Developing Countries and Economic Diplomacy

Owing to historical reasons the contemporary diplomatic practice and the principles of diplomacy were largely developed by the developed world. The issue is not whether these principles and practice are fair or unfair or whether they may be applied to the developing world at large. These principles and practice were developed at a time when the world was dominated largely by the colonial powers or other powers. But, these principles and practice are not to be rejected in their entirety; it should be borne in mind that the provisions in the Vienna Convention on Diplomatic Relations 1961 or the Vienna Convention on Consular Relations 1963 are, in general, acceptable. The issue of the inviolability of diplomatic bags or diplomatic missions have already been reviewed owing to a new practice developed by certain States based on the need for taking protective measures necessitated by the wave of international terrorism, and also for reviewing the practice of diplomatic immunity in relation to commercial acts.[1] This does suggest that diplomatic practice and principles thereto are reviewable and changeable too.

By the same token, the roles of international trade and private foreign investment need to be reviewed so as to strike a balance between the

[1] See, further H Fox and P Webb, *The Law of State Immunity*, 3rd edition, Oxford University Press (2013); I Sinclair, "The Law of State Immunity: Recent Developments", 167 *Hague Recueil* (1980); see also C Chatterjee, *International Law and Diplomacy*, op. cit., at 217–229.

C. Chatterjee, *Economic Diplomacy and Foreign Policy-making*,
https://doi.org/10.1007/978-3-030-49047-8_13

interest of developed and developing countries. For example, trade liberalisation in the true sense of the term is an issue which deserves further reviews. It has been explained in the Chapter entitled the "Focus of Economic Diplomacy" that the factors of trade liberalisation have not been correctly reviewed as yet, although UNCTAD has been making untiring efforts to achieve it. On the other hand, attitudes and perceptions of private foreign investors when investing in developing countries need to change in that the interests of developing countries in attaining economic self-sufficiency through efforts of the investors and direct participation of host countries in such investments must be enhanced.

It is to be emphasised that given the unprecedented changes that have been taking place in the business world, developing countries need to adopt significant changes in their trade and investment-related policy-making to tactics in diplomatic negotiations concerning socio-economic issues, and that the onus largely falls on them to initiate new ideas at international fora rather than maintaining that they lack bargaining power.

A common practice prevalent, in general, across the developing world has been that with the change of a government, almost all the policies of the former regime change. This practice creates uncertainty in the minds of foreign business entities, and in particular, private foreign investors. Any absence of continuity, predictability and reliability in governmental policies directly harm host countries in that foreign parties would lose their confidence in those countries. Thus, private foreign investment policies must be clearly stated, the procedures thereto must also be transparent, and the principle of State responsibility along with the observance of the international minimum standards, must be maintained. Abuse of sovereigns' inherent power expressed through administrative practices in the name of the "public interest" must be avoided. The cases in point are *BP v Libya* and *Texaco v Libya.*

In these cases, the host governments exercised their inherent sovereign power to compel the British and US private foreign investors to leave their countries. In the Libyan cases however, the Libyan act of taking assets was not only illegal but discriminatory. Not all developing host countries have abused their sovereign powers, but these examples will have a direct adverse impact on developing countries, in general.

On the other hand, the traditional attitudes of private foreign investors, in general, of profit maximisation, at the cost of the interests of host countries, need to be reviewed. Private foreign investors must also refrain from doing something which would harm the interest of developing countries, whether from a financial standpoint, or in regard to the protection of the environment or even in promoting child labour.

It falls on developing countries to vigorously initiate economic diplomacy of a new type which would create confidence, reliability and predictability in the minds of private foreign investors from the developed world. This is where the nexus between economic diplomacy and domestic policies and national standards becomes important. It may sound odd, but given the fact that diplomats are required to be engaged in diplomacy, they may be the best agents to initiate policy changes. It is appreciated that diplomats represent their sovereigns, but nevertheless, they are the agents who will encounter difficulties in striking good deals while engaged in economic diplomacy. In other words, the procedures for making domestic and foreign policies need to be reviewed.

Policy-making, whether on domestic or foreign policy-related issues, should be democratic and it must pay attention to the issue of good image-making in the wider world. This would suggest that all host countries in the developing world conform to the established principles of international law, namely the principle of State responsibility, the international minimum standard, a policy of providing protection to private foreign investors and maintain non-discriminatory treatment towards the private foreign investors.

But, most of all, a reliable and unbiased judicial system is a prerequisite for creating confidence in the minds of private foreign investors. The pride of national judiciaries in terms of their excellence becomes academic, when they are not allowed to consider politically-oriented legal issues pertaining to contracts, which are rooted in developing countries. This is an extremely important point for a successful economic diplomacy.

Economic diplomacy will meet with failure if the domestic systems are not based on the principles of democracy granting rights and freedoms to the people, and the administrative and judicial systems are not reliable. Diplomacy of the olden days and that in the fast-changing contemporary world are different.

The practice of maintaining what may be described as a never-ending bureaucracy combined with its attendant evils, and complex administrative procedure, even in regard to port clearances or customs clearances often hinder progress in economic diplomacy. Diplomats are not only the representatives of their sovereigns, but also, they are evaluated in reality, by reference to the countries to which they belong. Thus, in the case of diplomacy in general, and economic diplomacy, in particular, the legal principle that "all sovereigns are equal" is not honoured in reality. "Mutual gains" forms the basis for economic diplomacy, and the issue of establishing appropriate mutuality may not arise if the domestic systems create apprehension or doubts in the minds of the other parties. Economic diplomacy between developed countries and that between developing and developed countries are different in perception and in practice.

In order for them to have a successful economic relationship with foreign agencies in whatever form, developing countries are required to satisfy a significant number of conditions at a domestic level, such as effective legislation, including intellectual property legislation, banking, administrative framework, investment policy and above all an effective and prompt system of enforcing court orders.

Economic diplomacy or general diplomacy for that matter, are becoming, in essence, two types of diplomacy; developing countries, in general, are required to be in line with the diplomacy of the rich mainly by reforming the foundations of governance, the practice of non-transparency, the lack of democratic participatory governments, and the lack of accountability to societies. These are achievable. Thus, economic diplomacy at an international level has a direct relationship with the domestic policies of host States.

CHAPTER 14

The Role of Non-Governmental Organisations in Economic Diplomacy

14.1 Introduction

The term "non-governmental organisation" is rather broad; it may from a literal standpoint mean any organisation which is not "governmental", which may include any organisation of any nature, but which is not part of or associated with any public or governmental institutions. In the context of this work, a non-governmental institution would stand for that institution which acts as an "action group" and pursues wider socio-economic aims that may have a political dimension but they themselves are not political organisations or institutions. These types of organisations are often described as "civil society organisations" signifying that they operate for the civil society or promote causes for civil societies.

Non-governmental organisations can be of various sizes, and their impact on civil societies and on governments or international or inter-governmental organisations can vary from a qualitative point of view. The Oxfam International operates in about 100 countries with a combined annual income of £1 billion.[1] The size of these organisations is often determined by their objectives and funds they may use.

In view of the nature of the work they do, and the truly international objectives which form the foundation of such non-governmental organisations, some of them are known as International Non-Governmental

[1] See D Green and P Bloomer, "NGOs in Economic Diplomacy" in *The New Economic Diplomacy*, N Bayne and S Woolcock (eds), Farnham, Ashgate (2011) at 113.

C. Chatterjee, *Economic Diplomacy and Foreign Policy-making*,
https://doi.org/10.1007/978-3-030-49047-8_14

Organisations (INGOs), namely the International Red Cross, the headquarters of which is located in Geneva, Switzerland. A number of non-governmental bodies are faith-based, namely Christian Aid or Islamic Relief, while many others have limited objectives such as Water Aid. The limited scope of the objectives of a non-governmental organisation should not undermine its status.

Non-governmental organisations also exist in the commercial world, such as the national Chambers of Commerce or the International Chamber of Commerce in Paris, which is regarded as an international non-governmental organisation. Non-governmental organisations work as "action groups"; they directly contribute to creating public awareness. Action groups are not usually available or allowed to be set up in many non-democratic States.

This chapter attempts to examine critically the role of non-governmental organisations, in general, in economic diplomacy.

14.2 A Brief Account of the Historical Growth and Development of Non-Governmental Organisations

The purpose is not to accurately trace the beginning of non-governmental organisations in the world, but to identify and briefly explain some of the most important non-governmental organisations which proved to be relevant to international economic diplomacy, for example, anti-drug movements, abolition of slavery and slave trade, use of counterfeit currencies, environmental issues and import–export trade-related issues. Again, examples of some such organisations will be:

(a) The Anti-Opium Information Bureau in Geneva (which is no longer in existence);
(b) The World Alliance of YMCA (for their campaign against the suppression of illicit trade and traffic in drugs);
(c) International Conference of Catholic Charities;
(d) International Federation of Women Lawyers; and
(e) The International Chamber of Commerce in Paris.

The organisations at (b), (c) and (d) had been permitted to sit (without any right to make any statement, written and oral) at public meetings of the UN Conference for the Adoption of a Single Convention on Narcotic Drugs.

Currently, the list of non-governmental organisations engaged in numerous fields of activities is extremely long, starting with Amnesty International, Human Rights Action, organisations for the protection and preservation of the environment; Oxfam and so on. These organisations directly contribute to raising the level of public awareness in the field of activities in which they are engaged.

Diplomats should be allowed to interact with the relevant non-governmental organisations as their experience in particular area of activity may, in turn, enrich their knowledge rather than maintaining the old-fashioned idea that diplomats are mere functionaries of their higher authorities. Diplomacy is a discipline which in the contemporary period should be allowed to interact with the representations of external bodies too.

14.2.1 National Non-Governmental Organisations (NGOs)

Domestic NGOs are useful for a variety of reasons: (a) they promote their own cause within the national boundaries and lobby public authorities to demonstrate their "concern" on behalf of the civil society or their members before parliament or other relevant institutions; (b) they create public awareness in regard to specific issues coming under the purview of their objectives; (c) they become a formidable platform to present their views to protect the civil society, for example, certain calculated risks (environmental or health hazards) or unacceptable behaviours of business entities (promotion of smoking or alcohol consumption by manufacturers of these products) and (d) their activities do not aim at monetary profit-making.

These organisations may render two types of services at a national level: (a) presenting the views of the organisation in respect of domestic issues which the national or local government should review or abandon the plans altogether; in other words, these are attempts to oppose a governmental plan which according to them, would harm the civil society. Peaceful, firm and determined protests often can produce the desired results. NGOs must be recognised by the national public authorities concerned; (b) joint NGO activities on the same issue, if same ideas are shared between themselves can be effective; the concern of the civil society is forcefully presented before the national public authorities concerned.

Domestic NGOs' activities may be extended to include issues of "international concern". The best example to establish this point would be the abolition of the apartheid regime in South Africa in the 1970s. Such protests provide signals to the diplomatic world as to what kind of strategies it would adopt in dealing with an issue which has attained the status of an international concern. In other words, certain "concerns" at a domestic level may eventually progress into a matter of international concern; in fact, the foreign Missions in the receiving States may have to encounter protests and be prepared with their reactions to them through the local media. This in turn, provides momentum to the NGOs devoted to that cause in the country of origin, and sensible governments may like to pay heed to the aspirations of the local civil societies.

Domestic NGOs can form alliances with similar NGOs in different countries sharing similar ideas and policies in regard to specific issues. For example, trade union NGOs often form such alliances to protect the interests of employees by claiming minimum wages and/or guaranteeing them certain basic rights at places of work, namely health and safety-related rights, recess during the hours of work, or healthy environment in the workplace. The Trade Union Congress (TUC) in England is an example to endorse the strength of the labour movement not only at a national level but also across national boundaries. From this standpoint national/domestic NGOs may attain an international dimension by virtue of the nature of their activities.

Government malpractices are often highlighted by NGOs, and such activities often attain an international dimension. The movement against the use of nuclear weapons initiated by, among others, CND in the UK is worth mentioning. This movement has been very successful, and along with similar movements, helped the IAEA, the International Atomic Energy Association to promote this issue at an international level; indeed, although certain countries whether covertly or overtly still strengthen themselves with the lethal means of mass destruction, the movements initiated by NGOs in various countries have produced a high degree of deterrent to using these weapons. The movement by Greenpeace for prohibition of nuclear tests carried out by France in the South Pacific, which eventually led to referring the issue to the International Court of Justice,[2] by Australia and New Zealand. However, the World Health Organization (WHO) also sought an Advisory Opinion from the Court on the question of whether the use of nuclear weapons by a State in a war or other armed conflict be a breach of its obligations under international law including the WHO Constitution? According to the Court, although the question did not relate to any particular dispute, the Court, in view of the WHO's main objective which is "the attainment by all people of the highest possible level of health"; despite an absence of any question on the legality or illegality of the use of nuclear weapons it rendered its Advisory Opinion on the merits of the issue raised; and held, inter alia, that:

(a) neither customary law nor conventional law provides any specific authorisation of the threat or use of nuclear weapons;
(b) a threat of or the use of force by means of nuclear weapons is in breach of Article 2(4) of the UN Charter and which would also fail to satisfy the requirements of Article 51 of the UN Charter is unlawful.

It may be deduced from the above Advisory Opinion that the threat or use of nuclear weapons would generally be contrary to the rules of international law applicable to armed conflicts and the principles of international humanitarian law.

The anti-nuclear weapon movement developed an economic dimension—owing to international pressure brought to bear upon France predominantly by NGOs, France aborted the test series at the sixth test, but in view of the damage the tests inflicted on the region, global action ensued which culminated into, inter alia, boycotting of French wine and cheese. The Government of France gave an undertaking not to carry out further nuclear tests.

It is to be emphasised in this context that what originated as an NGO movement eventually culminated into a matter of "international concern" requiring the International Court of Justice to give a ruling on the issue.

Domestic NGOs dealing with commercial and financial issues can be very effective platforms for providing advice to governments, if so

[2] Nuclear Tests Case (Judgment) *New Zealand v France* [1979] ICJ Reports 457; see also Nuclear Tests Cases, *Australia v France*; *New Zealand v France* [1974] ICJ Reports 253.

requested by the latter, in the form of consultation papers or direct advice or internal research papers. Such NGOs are quite influential not only in the West but also in some of the non-Western countries. Most of the countries have their own Chamber of Commerce or other similar NGO dealing with specific issues. In the UK, for example, non-political and commercial or financial NGOs have influential voice in public affairs of an economic or a commercial nature—the London Chamber of Commerce, the Institute of Directors, the British Bankers' Association to name but a few. Governments in power, as a matter of practice, do seek their opinions, on appropriate issues.

These institutions can also form alliances across national boundaries with a view to achieving solidarity on chosen issues, particularly in regard to trade matters or governance of corporate entities or management of banks and finance houses or even about creation of new markets abroad. Harmonisation of regulations or practices between States on specific issues are also dealt with by such NGOs. Diplomats/Missions in receiving States should pay attention to the changes that may be forged in the field of commerce and trade by NGOs in order to initiate discussion, if necessary, with both the receiving State authorities and their respective domestic institutions and Ministries.

14.3 Non-Governmental and Inter-Governmental Organisations Engaged in Transnational Activities and Their Impact on International Economic Diplomacy

There are a number of non-governmental bodies whose activities have an international dimension and diplomats may not disregard their influence in developing elements of international economic diplomacy. One of the influential organisations under this category would be the International Chamber of Commerce which is located in Paris. Some of its works have been recognised by the international commercial community, namely UCP (Uniform Commercial Papers) which is revised from time to time and which is applied by the vast majority States when in import–export trade, payments are made through letters of credit; it has also developed guidelines as to import export trade done by e-commerce, in addition to publishing INCOTERMS (International Chamber of Commerce Terms) which govern carriage of goods by sea and details the rights of buyers, sellers and carriers of goods. Diplomats engaged in diplomacy are required to be familiar with these works in dealing with issues relating to import–export trade,[3] bearing in mind that governments are the largest buyers and sellers on the world markets. ICC has also developed works on trade terms, namely fob (free on board) and cif (costs, insurance and freight) and other terms which are used almost universally.

As stated earlier, economic diplomacy is concerned with issues and matters with an economic and commercial dimension, and it is through this form of diplomacy that either socially abominable issues might be dealt with effectively so that they cannot flourish, or what might be beneficial for the entire international community must be promoted by means of, where possible, binding instruments, namely resolutions or conventions or charter, etc.

Anti-Slavery International is a non-governmental NGO operating for over 160 years in order to abolish slavery and slave trade, which is still unfortunately rampant in the contemporary world. Here is another NGO whose activities have an international dimension. The organisation has not failed in its aims and objectives but unfortunately sufficient concerted action has not been taken as yet by the international community to make it a success. There is no need to explain or examine the purposes of this organisation; they are obvious, but they deserve an early attention of the international diplomatic community.

It is an issue with which economic diplomacy is directly concerned. The Anti-Slavery Convention of 1926[4] has failed directly implying that either it is not by an international convention that these acts may be effectively eradicated or that some of the governments have failed to place sufficient priority to these acts which have proved to be an illicit source of income at the cost of basic rights of human beings.

It would be beyond the remit of this work to go into details of what constitutes, for example, "slavery", but one of the ways of effectively dealing with this trade would be to brand those who are engaged in

[3] For a detailed discussion of these issues, see I Carr and P Stone, *International Trade Law*, London, Routledge (latest edition); see also Jason Chua, *Law of International Trade: Cross-Border Commercial Transactions*, London, Sweet & Maxwell (latest edition) and C Chatterjee, *Legal Aspects of Trade Finance*, London, Routledge (2006).

[4] This Convention was amended by a Protocol of 23 October 1953; but a Supplementary Convention on the Abolition of Slavery, Slave Trade, and Institutions and Practice Similar to Slavery was adopted in 1956.

this trade as "international criminals" and bring them to justice. It is through effective diplomacy at an international level that this issue should be urgently dealt with.

The International Criminal Police Organisation (INTERPOL) located in Lyon, France is an inter-governmental organisation which dealt with, inter alia, transnational crimes, including fraud, drug-trafficking, illicit arms deals, money laundering, slavery ad slave trade, etc. In order to effectively deal with such crimes, governments may find it useful to co-operate with INTERPOL in minimising the incidence of these crimes. It is primarily for the central criminal office (in whichever name it may be designated in a country) to liaise with INTERPOL. Dealing with economic or transnational crimes should be regarded as part of economic diplomacy, although in this context this form of diplomacy may not be constructed as a progressive diplomacy. Liaison with other countries and corresponding institutions would be essential for successfully carrying out this form of diplomacy. This should be regarded as a kind of preventive diplomacy for the purpose of taking preventative measures against international crimes. In this connection, security studies for diplomats may stand in good stead.

Non-governmental and inter-governmental organisations can directly contribute to the strengthening of a cause in which the international community has evidenced its political will. Again, during the 1970s, the anti-apartheid movement received an indomitable momentum from various non-governmental organisations too; one such organisation was the World Council of Churches located in Geneva. Apartheid in South Africa had an economic dimension too. The concerted efforts made by various countries at an international level with an active participation of diplomats and the determination of the United Nations combined with the active interest taken by the World Council of Churches, in addition to various other non-governmental organisations at all levels of the international community brought the end of the apartheid regime in South Africa.

14.4 Challenges to Be Met by NGOs

NGOs usually meet challenges from two sources: (a) internal; and (b) external. Internal challenges are mostly, if not entirely, created by the internal political system which would prevent setting up of any action groups or non-governmental bodies, in case it encounters challenges from these institutions. Such policies are self-defeating in that it is often believed that it might help to create undeclared groups which may develop strategies for overthrowing the regime or accumulates pent-up dissatisfaction towards the regime which might culminate into a resolution against the regime.

Rebel groups may not be confused with NGOs. These groups which would eventually form alliance with similar groups overseas for various kinds of help, including supply of arms and ammunitions or even security-related intelligence, would not be endowed with the purposes and characteristics of NGOs. However, these groups, during the initial period of their activities may appear to be NGOs but they are, in effect, pseudo NGOs. NGOs are not usually allowed to be set up in non-democratic regimes, and this policy largely contributes to creating rebel groups, but various other reasons may also contribute to the setting up of rebel groups within a country.

In their real forms, NGOs' principal functions would be to bring about, by peaceful dialogues with various regimes, ineffective or inefficient socio-economic policies within countries and to operate as mouthpieces for civil societies to make and retain regimes democratic allowing the peoples in a society their basic rights and freedoms. These objectives may not know any boundaries. Socio-economic policies have a variety of dimensions; as stated earlier, it is through dialogues and democratic processes that these policies should be improved. Democratic governments should invite NGOs to ensure that their governance receives the approval of their electorate, and if this is not done, then NGOs will meet challenges and governments will be subject to even more challenges too, a prelude to a chaotic society and governance.

The more internal challenges an action group or NGO may receive, the more external help these groups and NGOs will seek; eventually, the regime's own position will be questionable and become weak. This is where "internal diplomacy" should come into play in a constructive fashion whereby a meaningful co-operation between the regime and action groups and/or NGOs would develop. A chaotic regime must be avoided for averting any further chaos in a given society. In a chaotic regime, the first casualty is usually the sacrifice of a stable economy, and inevitably further consequences arising from economic instability will ensue. Internal diplomacy with the participation of internal officers is as important as external diplomacy for the stability of a regime.

Encounters with the regime should be avoided, where possible. A high degree of "informal" rather than "formal" "backstage" working relationship should be developed between action groups/NGOs and the political establishment. Such tactics and strategies prove to be more effective than any formal citizen-state engagement.[5] Diplomacy is about negotiation based on the "tool" called skills—understanding of the basic issues; understanding of the other party's strategies and goals; striking a balance of interests; protection of the interests of the domestic communities and lessening of tensions. A friendly environment combined with a genuine intention to diffuse the problem-related tension. A dictatorial attitude and conduct on the part of either party will be doomed to failure. Thus, the internal challenges should be met by action groups/NGOs in an amiable fashion rather than heightening the tension. Action groups/NGOs also need diplomatic skills in participating in a negotiation process. It is primarily through the internal processes where possible that the internal differences should be ironed out.

External challenges may come through interventionary processes, that is, when external bodies may, often without legitimacy, intervene in certain others' domestic issues. In the anti-apartheid movement in South Africa, which had an economic dimension, effectively became a matter of "international concern", the investors failed to provide support to the movement for obvious reasons. It virtually turned out to be a conflict between "conscience and monetary gains", but in view of a formidable international political will demonstrated through various non-governmental organisations, internal and external combined with the indomitable determination of the United Nations as well as political will manifested particularly by India, Zambia and Zimbabwe, the internal opposition eventually proved to be futile.

External challenges often have their own narrow motives—to defeat a noble cause at a national level. These may often be fomented by the internal regime concerned. External challenges amount to "interventions" in the domestic affairs of the intervened State. In such cases, interventions usually take place with the consent of the internal authority. The objectives of NGOs will in such circumstances be defeated. NGOs are not supposed to unite to be engaged in warfares, but they may be

[5] See further J Garenta and R McGee (eds), *Citizen Action and National Policy: Making Change Happen*, London, Zed Books (2010); see also J Howell and J Pearce, *Civil Society and Development; A Critical Exploration*, Boulder (2001).

united (alliances) with other NGOs to make their position formidable. But, any protest they wish to make must be peaceful and non-violent.

NGOs may be subject to external challenges if they themselves exceed their remit of activities or intervene in the internal affairs of a State. Challenges from external sources may be formidable. In order to avoid challenges of any nature, internal or external, NGOs should try to integrate themselves into the local society, so that the civil society may be an ally and they receive support from them.

In order for foreign NGOs to work in a foreign jurisdiction, NGO staff should be familiar with the local socio-economic issues, administrative and governmental policy issues and above all the local language. Foreign authorities should also appreciate the objectives which NGOs in their countries would like to perform, and co-operate with them to achieve the objectives in the interests of the local people and the communities.

14.5 NGOs' Scope and Method of Work

In relation to economic diplomacy, NGOs' role may not necessarily be kept confined to the originating country. Purely domestic NGOs' activities are almost exclusively confined to the country concerned in which they might originate; but the nature of their activities might require them either to locate them in strategically important locations or establish contacts with other relevant NGOs outside of their home country.

However, with the changing world in respect of almost all spheres of human life, NGOs now often participate in activities which would influence public policy and even the activities of transnational corporations or even international institutions concerned with the protection of the environment or peoples' rights and freedoms, trade liberalisation or even international immigration. By virtue of the quality of their work they may be allowed to attend the relevant institutions as "observers" (without the right to vote), where possible.

An NGO's success often depends upon its grass-root level work which broadens their outlook and a thorough understanding of the problems and issues, and of course, advocacy bearing in mind that they would encounter formidable opposition from the law-makers or even from internal and external sources. Both lobbying and advocacy are now established methods of making NGOs' voices heard. As stated earlier, good quality research combined with campaign and media coverage and the creation of public awareness on an international level usually prove to be an effective image-building activity which is essential for making its voice heard. Alliances often prove to be helpful in promoting global movement for social justice.[6]

NGOs' movement concerning certain issues should provide signals to diplomats what is on the horizon, what strategies they should adopt to maintain social justice or on what grounds the ideas advocated by the NGOs may be opposed. On the other hand, NGOs' agenda might facilitate resolving any differences by conciliation and negotiation. Diplomats should not perceive NGOs as their enemies; co-operation with them might be helpful for both the parties. However, diplomats may find it useful to develop their strategies in the following way which have been developed by Oxfam, a very well-known NGO with an international dimension, as its internal guidelines:

- To define objectives; in so doing to create room for flexibility and change, and if so, the nature of changes and obstacles, if any, to change. Cost–benefit analysis particularly in regard to the proposed changes; the obstacles to change which may be prejudice, political, and that changes would not be possible to make in the circumstances or that from a diplomatic or practical perspective changes would not be viable.
- To define targets; only achievable targets should be identified, and ascertain who may be the decision-makers, and the level of bureaucracy; who has formal and informal powers; who has a decisive influence on a decision-making process; what kind of precautionary measures should be taken to ensure that the decision does not become negative in form. It might be useful to seek an informal interview with the authorities concerned to test the water; this would help diplomats to know in advance what the NGOs wish to achieve.
- To determine tools to influence targets; research, lobbying, publicity seek advice from key advisers, criticism and strengths already available, opinions of the relevant eminent people, academics, public officials, parliamentarians, business associations, trade unions, consumers' and stakeholders' opinions.

[6] D Green and P Bloomer, op. cit., at 119.

14.6 Conclusions

NGOs serve a very constructive service to societies and the international community on important issues with which civil societies and governmental and international organisations are involved. These organisations are neutral and work without any bias in favour of or against anybody or any institution. Their objectives are clear—to transform unjust into just. This is not motivated by any individual's value judgement; it is an institutional judgement based on research and to conform to aspirations of particular societies or the international community.

NGOs are not profit-making institutions; their cause is to promote welfare and correct the incorrect or to provide help to those who deserve it. They are not "judgmental" institutions; they are concerned with "actions" for remedial measures. It may be maintained that these organisations function on human follies and misconduct.

The nexus between NGOs and INGOs and diplomatic communities should be a close one rather than one of conflicts or disagreements. It has been explained in this chapter that a responsible diplomatic community should not aggravate a situation; a close working relationship with NGOs and INGOs can be very productive in settling differences arising from particular issues. This procedure can be described as "preventative diplomacy", a method of avoiding conflicts.

NGOs work for people or issues which may have adverse impact on societies or the international community at large. Co-operation between NGOs and diplomats may simply find a non-conflictual solution of an issue of a domestic nature or an international issue. It is to be emphasised that in view of the quality of their activities, certain of the NGOs and INGOs have been accorded the status of "observers" by the United Nations and its specialised agencies.

NGOs are not law-making bodies, but these organisations can initiate new legislation or international conventions, where necessary, which will of course be taken up by governments or the relevant international organisations to adapt, respectively. Economic diplomacy is a form of diplomacy which requires "listening to" others; NGOs are to be listened to. NGOs ad INGOs directly contribute to creating public awareness of issues of concern for domestic and international communities.

Conclusions

It has been emphasised in writing this work that in view of the changing nature of economic diplomacy, diplomats are now required to be fully equipped with knowledge and training in a variety of disciplines. Economic diplomacy's primary objective is to develop economic relationship in chosen countries on a bi-lateral diplomacy basis and also to develop new principles at an international level which would be shared by all States in conducting economic diplomacy.

In order to develop and strengthen the foundations of economic relations when on a bi-lateral or multilateral basis, what is most needed is a thorough understanding of the functional aspects of sovereignty rather than maintaining the need for application of any rigid form of sovereignty.

Among other qualities, diplomats are required to be competent negotiators. It has been emphasised in this work that there is no room for "bargaining power" in proper negotiations; "bargaining power" stands for the "power to negotiate", but one cannot effectively negotiate anything, unless one has a thorough knowledge in the subject matter of a negotiation. But, of course, a negotiation process will be one-sided, when one side is dependent on the other party by virtue of being a borrower. Unfortunately, this is the situation in which the vast majority of developing States are, in consequence of which they are dominated by the lender countries and are unable to let their voice heard at the UN level.

C. Chatterjee, *Economic Diplomacy and Foreign Policy-making*,
https://doi.org/10.1007/978-3-030-49047-8

It has also been stressed in this work that by changing the foreign investment procedures currently operational in the majority of the developing States, they may be able to turn around their economics by paying attention to the development of their human resources (capacity building) by introducing BOT (Build, Operate and Transfer) system and buy-back condition in their investment contracts.

It is unfortunate that not many effectively operational regional economic organisations exist in the developing world. This is an issue which deserves their urgent attention, as by having these arrangements they should be able to increase their interregional trade on a mutually agreed concessional basis and exchange scientific information between themselves to enrich their research-bases to become inventive and innovative; economic diplomacy's objectives at a national level are to enrich States' economics by bi-lateral means and to develop their human resources too.

In so far as regional economic organisations as a factor of socio-economic development are concerned, one may cite ASEAN (The Association of South-East Asian Nations) as a generally successful regional economic organisation. There are certain obvious merits of such organisations: (a) they deepen friendship between the Member States through trade, investment and related activities between/among them; (b) secure economic and defence securities; and (c) which would gradually and eventually help solve the internal conflicts, if any, among themselves.

Developing States are required to appreciate that unless their enormous resources, both natural and human, in general, are exploited effectively to strengthen their economic position and gradually become major exporting countries; they will be looked down upon by the richer States and will remain aid-dependants forever. It is a changeable phenomenon, and they should pay their attention to it; otherwise, they will remain as former colonised States implying that they are sovereign States but in name only. Creation of interdependency between the developed and developing States is one of the main objectives of economic diplomacy.

However, none of these may be achieved unless the developed States have grown confidence in the developing States, and to achieve this goal, the latter need to do the following: (a) by making their governance system democratic, where necessary; (b) by developing appropriate policies and legislation for the protection of foreign investments in accordance with the principles and standards of public international law; (c) by improving and developing confidence in their judicial system; (d) by separating the judiciary from the executive division of the government; (e) by according equal treatment to all and by guaranteeing their fundamental rights; and (f) by allowing non-governmental bodies to work with their government, where relevant. Whether a country needs attention to these issues may only be considered by the country herself. Here is the correlationship between domestic policies of a State and its position in promoting economic diplomacy.

In addition to what has been stated above, developing States may also like to pay attention to the following: (a) their banking and insurance systems; (b) the education system; (c) port system; and (d) human capacity building system. The domestic strengths of a country are a factor for being involved in economic negotiations with other States. Finally, another objective of economic diplomacy is to progressively decrease economic dependency, and concomitantly develop meaningful economic interdependency (a direct symptom of economic co-operation between States) which would eventually form the bases for peaceful co-existence and minimise the need for warfares of any nature between States. This is the reason why economic interaction between nations started in the olden days, and that reason is still valid, and indeed operational between and among the modern States. By the same token, an effective economic diplomacy is extremely relevant to small States which in the absence of any meaningful economic co-operation in the form of pulling of resources among themselves in the same geographic region and working together will only determine their standing in the world.

Incidentally, in this work, the terms "developed" and "developing" States have been used maintaining their popular meaning; it is appreciated that no accurate definitions of these two terms exist.

Bibliography and Additional Reading

Books

Blackhurst, R	"The WTO and the Global Economy", 20 *World Economy* (1997) 527–544.
Cable, V	*The Storm: The World Economic Crisis & What It Means*, London, Atlantic Books (2010).
Cambridge Advanced Learner's Dictionary	Cambridge, Cambridge University Press (Third Edition) (2008).
Carr, I and Stone, P	*International Trade Law*, London, Routledge (2018).
Chatterjee, C	*International Law and Diplomacy*, London, Routledge (2007).
———	*Legal Aspects of Trade Finance*, London, Routledge (2006).
Floud, R	*The People and the British Economy*, Oxford, Oxford University Press (1997).
Fox, H and Webb, P	*The Law of State Immunity*, Oxford, Oxford University Press (2013).

C. Chatterjee, *Economic Diplomacy and Foreign Policy-making*,
https://doi.org/10.1007/978-3-030-49047-8

Gaventa, J and McGee, R (eds) — *Citizen Action and National Policy: Making Change Happen*, London, Zed Books (2010).

Green, D and Bloomer, P — "NGOs in Economic Diplomacy" in N Bayne and S Woolcock (eds) *New Economic Diplomacy*, Farnham, Ashgate (2011).

Hirchman, A O — *The Strategy of Economic Development*, New Haven, Yale University Press (1958).

Howell, J and Pearce, J — *Civil Society and Development: A Critical Exploration*, Boulder (2001).

Jackson, J H — *The World Trade Organization: Constitution and Jurisprudence*, London, The Royal Institute of International Affairs (Latest Edition).

Kaplinsky, R — *Globalisation, Poverty and Inequality*, Cambridge, UK, Polity Press (2005).

Kostecki, M and Naray, O — *Commercial Diplomacy and International Business*, The Netherlands Institute for International Relations (2007).

Krueger, A O (ed) — *The WTO as an International Organization*, Chicago (1998).

League of Nations — *Commercial Policy in the Inter-War Period: International Proposals and National Policies* (1942).

Lee, D and Ruel, H — "Introduction: Commercial Diplomacy and International Business" in H Ruel (ed) *Commercial Diplomacy and International Business: A Conceptual and Empirical Exploration*, Emerald Publishing (2012).

Lester, B, Mercurio, B and Davis, A — *World Trade Law: Text Materials and Commentary*, Oxford, Hart Publishing (Latest Edition)

Maddison, A — *Monitoring the World Economy 1820–1992*, OECD Development Centre (1995).

Maull, H (ed) — *Germany's Uncertain Power: Foreign Policy of the Berlin Republic* (New Perspectives in German Political Studies), London, Palgrave Macmillan (2006).

Mehmet, O — *Westernizing the Third World*, London, Routledge (1999).

Murray, C, Holloway, D and Timpson Hunt, D — *Schmitthoff: The Law and Practice of International Trade*, London, Sweet & Maxwell (Latest Edition).

Naray, O — *Commercial Diplomacy: A Conceptual Overview*, A Paper presented at the 7th World Conference of TPOs, The Hague (2008).

North, D — *Institutions, International Change and Economic Performance*, Cambridge, Cambridge University (1990).

Ozden, M I — *Governmental Agencies in Commercial Diplomacy: Seeking the Optional Agency Structure of Foreign Trade Policy*, Raleigh, North Carolina State University (2009).

Pigman, G — *Contemporary Diplomacy*, London, Polity Press (2010).

Rana, K S — *21st Century Diplomacy*, The Continuum International Publishing Group (2011).

Rostow, W W — *The Stages of Economic Growth: A Non-Communist Manifesto*, Cambridge, Cambridge University Press (1960).

Ruel, H — *Commercial Diplomacy and International Business: A Conceptual and Empirical Exploration*, Emerald Group Publishing Ltd (2012).

Sinclair, I	"The Law of State Immunity: Recent Developments", 167 *Hague Recueil* (1980).
The World Bank	*Capacity Building in Africa: An OECD Evaluation of World Bank Support*, Washington DC (2005).
Van Den Bossche, P	*The Law and Policy of the World Trade Organization*, Cambridge, Cambridge University Press (Latest Edition).
White, G	*Nationalisation of Foreign Property*, Steven & Sons (1961).
Wilcox, C A	*A Charter of World Trade*, New York, Macmillan (1949).
World Trade Organization	*From GATT to the WTO: The Multilateral Trading System in the New Millennium*, The Hague, WTO and Kluwer Law International.
———	*A Handbook on the WTO Dispute Settlement System*, Cambridge, Cambridge University Press (2011).
Wortley, B	*Expropriation in Public International Law*, Cambridge, Cambridge University Press (1959).
UNCTAD	Draft Code of Conduct on Transfer of Technology (1985).
UN Department of Economic and Social Affairs	The Doha Declaration (2008).
United Nations	Transnational Corporations in World Development (1983).

Articles

Beattie, A	"US Says China and India put Trade Talks in Jeopardy", *The Financial Times*, 28 July 2008.

Bhagwati, J	"Splintering and Disembodiment of Services and Developing Nations" 7 *World Economy* (1984) 133–143.
Chatterjee, C	"The Reality of Risks in Private Foreign Investment", *International Company and Commercial Law Review* (1996).
———	"The Convention Establishing the Multilateral Investment Guarantee Agency", 36 *International and Comparative Quarterly* (1987) 76.
———	"Forty Years of International Action for Trade Liberalization" 23 *Journal of World Trade* (1989) at 45.
———	"The Charter of Economic Rights and Duties of States: An Evaluation after Fifteen Years" 40 *International and Comparative Law Quarterly* (1991) 669–684.
———	"From Doha to Cancún: A Multilateral Trading System?" 54 *Amicus Curiae* (2004).
———	"The MERCOSUR: A Model for Regional Economic Integrations" 101 *Amicus Curiae* (2015).
Chatterjee, S K	"International Law of Development", *Encyclopaedia for Comparative Public Law and International Law* (1986).
Dolzer, R	"Fair and Equitable Treatment: A Key Standard in Investment Treaties", 39 *International Law* (2005) 87.
Gould, P R	"Tanzania, 1920–1963: The Spatial Impress of the Modernization Process", 22 *World Politics* (1970) 149–170.
Hornbeck, S K	"The Most-favoured Nation Clause (Part I)", 3 *American Journal of International Law* (1909) 395–422.
Hoyle, B S	"African Socialism and Urban Development: The Relocation of the Tanzanian

Capital", *Tijdschrift voor Economische en Sociale Geografie* (1979) 207–216.

International Law Commission — Report on the Most-favoured Nation Standard (1969) vol II, UN Doc. A/CN.4/213.

Johnson, D H N — "The Binding Force of a Recommendation of the General Assembly of the United Nations", 32 *British Year Book of International Law* (1955–1956) 97.

Leinbach, T R — "The Spread of Modernisation in Malaya, 1895–1969", *Tijdschrift voor Economische en Sociale Geografie* (1972) 262–277.

Lindquist, J — "Tanzania: Socialist Ideology, Bureaucratic Reality, and Development far Below" in W B Stöhr and D R Taylor (eds) *Development from Above or Below?* Chichester, Wiley (1981) 329–349.

Nicolaides, P — "Towards Multilateral Rules on Competition: The Problems in Mutual Recognition of National Rules" 17 *World Competition* (1994) 5–48.

Palmer, D, MacInnis, L — "G4 Talks Collapse, Throw Trade Round into Doubt", *Reuters*, 21 June 2007.

Safir, M — "Towards the Definition of Patterns in the Distribution of Economic Development over East Africa", 7 *East Africa Geographic Review* (1969) 1–13.

Schwarzenberger, G — "The Most-favoured Nation Standard in British Practice", 22 *British Year Book of International Law* (1945) 96–121.

——— — "The Principles and Standards of International Economic Law", *Recueil des Cours*, The Hague Academy of International Law (1966) I, 1–98.

Sloan, B — "The Binding Force of a Recommendation of the General Assembly of the

United Nations", 25 *British Year Book of International Law* (1948) 14.

Vasciannie, S — "The Fair and Equitable Treatment Standard in International Law and Practice" 70 *British Year Book of International Law* (1998) 99.

Cases cited

Luther v Sagar [1921] 1 KB 456.
The SS Wimbledon (1923), PCIJ, Series A, No. 1.
Territorial Jurisdiction of the International Commission of the River Oder, PCIJ, Series A, (1929) at 27.
BP-Libya (Arbitration) 53 *International Law Reports* (1973, 1974) 297.
Nuclear Test Cases—New Zealand v France (1979) ICJ Reports 457; see also Australia v France; New Zealand v France [1974] ICJ Reports 253.
Texaco-Libya (Arbitration) 17 *International Legal Materials* (1978) 1.
Liamco-Libya (Arbitration) 20 *International Legal Materials* (1981) 1.
The Government of the State of Kuwait and the American Independent Oil Company (AMINOIL), 21 *International Legal Materials* (1982) 976.
Asian Agricultural Products Ltd v Sri Lanka, 30 *International Legal Materials* (1991) 577.
Minority Schools in Albania, PCIJ (1935) Series A/B No. 64.
Corfu Channel, ICJ Reports (1949) 4.

Documents Referred to

1. UN General Assembly Resolution entitled Permanent Sovereignty over Natural Resources (1962) 1803 (XVII) https://legal.un.org/avl/ha/ga_1803/ga_1803.html.
2. The New International Economic Order (1974) https://en.wikipedia.org/wiki/New_International_Economic_Order.
3. The Charter of Economic Rights and Duties of States (1974) https://legal.un.org/avl/ha/cerds/cerds.html.
4. Agreement between the Government of the United Kingdom of Great Britain and Northern Ireland and the Government of the Oriental Republic of Uruguay for the Promotion and Protection of

Investments, 1991 https://treaties.un.org/Pages/LatestVolumes.aspx?clang=_en Volume 2004 I-34348.
5. Agreement between the Government of Korea and the Government of the Republic of the Philippines for the Promotion and Protection of Investments, 1994 https://treaties.un.org/Pages/LatestVolumes.aspx?clang=_en Volume 2032 I-35081.
6. Agreement between the Government of Mongolia and the Government of the Kingdom of Denmark concerning the Promotion and Reciprocal Protection of Investments, 1996 https://treaties.un.org/Pages/LatestVolumes.aspx?clang=_en Volume 2009 I-34469.
7. Agreement between the Government of the Kingdom of Denmark and the Government of the Russian Federation concerning the Promotion and Reciprocal Protection of Investments, 1996 https://treaties.un.org/Pages/LatestVolumes.aspx?clang=_en Volume 2009 I-34468.

For 4 to 7 all agreements should be available in the **UN Treaty Series** in the relevant volumes shown above.

Index

C. Chatterjee, *Economic Diplomacy and Foreign Policy-making*,
https://doi.org/10.1007/978-3-030-49047-8

The manufacturer's authorised representative in the EU is Springer Nature Customer Service Centre GmbH, Europaplatz 3, 69115 Heidelberg, Germany. If you have any concerns regarding our products, please contact ProductSafety@springernature.com

Printed and bound by CPI Group (UK) Ltd, Croydon, CR0 4YY
30/09/2026
02225649-0003